Dying to Live

ADDING ZEAL TO LIFE

BHATUPE MHANGO-CHIPANTA

BALBOA.PRESS

A DIVISION OF HAY HOUSE

Balboa Press books may be ordered through booksellers or by contacting:

Balboa Press
A Division of Hay House
1663 Liberty Drive
Bloomington, IN 47403
www.balboapress.com
844-682-1282

Because of the dynamic nature of the Internet, any web addresses or links contained in this book may have changed since publication and may no longer be valid. The views expressed in this work are solely those of the author and do not necessarily reflect the views of the publisher, and the publisher hereby disclaims any responsibility for them.

The author of this book does not dispense medical advice or prescribe the use of any technique as a form of treatment for physical, emotional, or medical problems without the advice of a physician, either directly or indirectly. The intent of the author is only to offer information of a general nature to help you in your quest for emotional and spiritual well-being. In the event you use any of the information in this book for yourself, which is your constitutional right, the author and the publisher assume no responsibility for your actions.

This work is nonfiction. However, please note that the author has taken artistic liberty to change some names and places so as to avoid direct reference to real personalities and locations in an effort to preserve the integrity of these events as she recalls them. Any resemblance or similarity to any person dead or alive is unintended.

Scripture quotations marked NIV are taken from the Holy Bible, New International Version®. NIV®. Copyright © 1973, 1978, 1984 by International Bible Society. Used by permission of Zondervan. All rights reserved. [Biblica]

Print information available on the last page.

ISBN: 978-1-9822-6017-0 (sc)
ISBN: 978-1-9822-6018-7 (e)

Balboa Press rev. date: 12/18/2020

Dedication

To my son.

To "Mrs V". Or mom. Thank you for your guidance-not
only in the years we were blessed by your queenly presence
in this world but especially since you've been gone.

And to the millions who lived with, died of, and are
living with HIV and many other chronic conditions
around the globe; our lives, and stories, matter.

"I will not die, but live, and will proclaim what the Lord has done. He has chastened me severely, but he has not given me over to death."

-Psalm 118:17-18, [1]

---

[1] The Bible, New International Version

Contents

Introduction

One of the questions I get, besides: what kind of sex life do you have? Is "how did you get HIV-what's your story?" There was a time I would proceed to answer by giving up all the cringy details of how at age 22 I came to be diagnosed with an HIV-positive status. It was only in my 2nd year with the UN in global advocacy work, at the highest international levels, that it finally clicked that the question folks were really asking me, but not quite properly articulating, was *"how in the world can it be that a young, vibrant, educated, unmarried, globe-trotting woman like you happened to get this virus?"* This question, I unpacked to be laden with all kinds of stigmas, myths and misinformation, making me out to be some outlier to the demographic that they thought contracts HIV. It was after this sudden realization that I opted to toughen my stance as a PLHIV[2]. You see, for so long I believed the world was accustomed to statistics on "those infected", "communities of people living with HIV", gay men, people with multiple sexual partners, sex workers who contracted HIV during their risky jobs, the percentages shared on CNN news and BBC radio shows and other media houses of how this epidemic was spreading around the globe. There was definitely also a preoccupation with the sexualization of the pandemic, as if this were the only means of spread. This narrative of classifying these groups or making them seem "other", sadly, I came to learn in global activism efforts, was and remains a key contributor to the existing high rates of stigmatization of people living with this infection (and might I add, other vices). It's so effective in the sense that people build fake narratives of what these "other" people are like, never imagining for a second that they could possibly cross paths with such a person, outside of a visit to a brothel, the wrong end of town, a sex shop- not that any of these places in themselves are an automatic window into HIV transmission. In fact, the fallacy in such an image is so profound and was proved by studies across Africa years ago that showed married and sexually-faithful people succumbing to this epidemic, as the rate of increase of sero-discordant couples became a real

---

[2] Person Living with HIV, an acronym coined in HIV advocacy work to refer to all those infected with HIV.

thing. There was so much moralization of the epidemic. PLHIVs, myself included, have for decades shared how we are all not a monolithic whole, that we each are not a number, but a singularly-affected, human individual with particular quirks, interests and a backstory. In my years of advocacy work I met many PLHIVs with stories more wonderfully varied and layered than my own. There is for instance the elderly european man, who learned of his HIV-positive status as a grandfather, when he wanted to donate blood to a friend. There is the young, but asexual guy who learned of his HIV positive status at a Needle exchange program during his drug-using days. There is the west african "sister" Whose husband beat up and threw out of their family home their family home after getting results of an unauthorized HIV test that never should have happened in the first place! There is the blonde eastern european woman who lost her baby early on and soon after learning of its and her HIV positive status. I could go on all day long. I've never packaged these stories into bizarre and "other", but seen them as just another part of the human experience that some get to walk through. I've always seen these "HIV victims" as people, as I know I myself am no victim, but a person. I know people. HIV positive people. I myself am one, and have never felt ashamed to be a part of this global group that is as powerful as it is colourful and varied, like a box of crayons. As we are all so different, I can't share one single story of the HIV positive experience. I can only most vividly share my own. Moralizing HIV never worked and will never help the world to cope with this or any other global, viral epidemic. Asking questions to gather a sense of whether folks were innocent or guilty in how they contracted this infection will never take us beyond the myths. No, we are all in this together: the tested and positive, the tested and negative, the-afraid-to test, the-never-been-tested, and the-never-will-test. I see us all as being on a continuum of status and we are all connected. We are not to be seen as victims, or numbers, but as humans that can host viruses that are out there seeking to occupy new territory. Yes, it sounds a bit clinical. But, I reckon this dry view may be the only one that can keep us humane, caring, preventative in habits and focused on the future, compared to other perspectives.

My point? Many people are unprepared to find an openly HIV positive person standing healthily before them, sharing their same space, using their amenities and even thriving in their world. At least this has been my experience. In my now 18 years of living with HIV I have found that beyond caring for others enough to educate them on this virus and the positive status, I've had to also manage their shock and surprise and continue to make my face and voice seen and heard, where appropriate. The result has been a most colourful life, full of memorable moments and stories worth recounting over and over to those near and dear. But it wasn't always like this. It's also been tough, for I've had at times to set aside my own emotions so as to care for another through disclosures that led to disastrous results for me. As God has blessed me dearly, with a life enriched with a family, many friends and fulfilling passions, I thought it only suitable that I in turn share some key lessons gathered over these near 2 decades of my enigmatic existence. In a few years, if I am to continue to stay alive, taking my life-long anti-retroviral medication I will have lived almost half my life with HIV. Incredible! Who would have thought?

It's a given: a lot has changed in the social and global landscape since I learned of my positive diagnosis in 2002. SARS, Ebola, and now the Corona Virus are actually global phenomena as scary and as catastrophic as HIV and AIDS were once feared as being, and yet all with even faster rates of mortality. But its early days for the Covid19, and scientific reports and predictions prove it could be way more fatal in a short time than AIDS ever was. And yet each of these new viral sensations affect humans mostly just by direct contact with an infected person, and yet HIV requires one to have real, almost intimate interaction with an infected human being. In 2020 we are living in a small global village in which we are all inundated with information- real and fake. Sorting through the rubbish to get to the truth at times, for many people is too much work. So, I find much has changed, but a lot of the old myths about HIV and AIDS remain stuck in the minds of many.

If you are like many across the globe, you're glued to the news channels, browsing internet pages and searching for answers to the violent storm that's sweeping across nations; that of the corona virus pandemic or #Covid19 as it's now registered in various social media platforms. What have you lost? Yet another more important question you'll have to answer is what have you gained? That's where all the opportunity lies, where we find all the strength to keep on going, despite negative news stories and fears of the future. The popular saying that *"sometimes, we stare so long and hard at the slammed door that we don't recognize the cracked window opening right before us"* rings true at moments like now. People who weren't the best of parents think back to better times with their children, pathetic lovers dream only of being with their loved ones, folks who hated their jobs nonetheless romanticize office hours they will never get back. It's normal. As humans, we can and do at times take much for granted. And we can and do at times go "through the motions", barely aware of our own existence, but ticking off tasks and to-do lists. In fact, many of us are like zombies; sleepwalking through the parts of life we hate, and smiling at the appropriate moments. We've all been on the planet's go-go-go pace for so long, but Covid19 forces us all to slow down, be present, be still, lean on each other, express our fears, be awake. But what does it mean to be fully awake to the enormity of life, and living?! This is the crux and sum of my story, and the reason I write this book. I've found that to let myself be surprised by the eventualities of life has been to-date so much more rewarding than sitting on the sidelines, wondering how much better life would have been if not for HIV. I've had to lay aside my expectations and let the gravity of life pull me through all these past years.

Today, it's Covid19 at our doorstep. I wrote this book well ahead of this scourge but as it silently rages around the world I implore you to do one thing: be fully present in the demands of your day, but don't forget to look AHEAD, plan AHEAD, think AHEAD, even as I do the same. What's gone is behind us. All we have now is what we are going to do with the rest of our lives. How are we going to show up in the world? What legacy do we wish to leave behind? And, finally, how have our past experiences, adventures and even failures prepared us for this moment? We must list them. Embrace them. Celebrate them! And, please do let's buckle up. Life is such a bumpy ride!

Of course I am not all about the gloom and doom. I've always believed there is more to life than just exhaling the air, breathing an existence. Am all about the fly, fun and fab…, all about the living! So, grab a snack, curl up in your cosy nook and walk in my shoes for a bit.

PART 1

Chapter 1

My Mother had a name

The year was 1987. The city was Maputo, Mozambique. Yes, back then war-torn Mozambique was both still a beautiful vacation destination for foreigners and an inescapable nightmare for many locals. You see, between 1977 and 1992 there existed a huge war between the RENAMO and FRELIMO. [At the time in Mozambican history the country was led by the Frelimo party but slowly its rather communist dealings did not sit well with some members of this party, who broke off and set up an anti-communist grouping, that is now an official political party, Renamo. The war went on til about 1992 when a peace pact was signed by the two warring sides. (Google it!) Yet here we were, one fine sunny saturday morning- my mother, sisters and I, tossing our suitcases into the back of a minivan. My mom would later take the wheel and tell us we had two more house stops at her friends to collect the rest of our "travel party". My mother was then working for the Malawi Embassy in Mozambique. She had moved into this position and country just a year before but had already picked up quite the name as a socialite and with her title had gotten under her belt already a couple of other high-powered socialite friends. Together they organized so many indoor and outdoor gatherings for themselves and their kids (us) and slowly we had begun to have a community form around us. There was Aunt Kutwalno, from Botswana, a lady we could count on to always bring the best foodstuff that just got through the south african border (hello, Tennis biscuits, hello Biltong!). There was Aunt Mercy, a Ugandan no-nonsense woman who always shared her latest african fashions with my mother, and that trickled down to us in the house. Then there was my mom's favourite Mozambican woman, a Xangani woman who was infatuated with Portuguese men and who probably drank *cerveja* every waking day of her life, I think. She was a lot of fun and owned a range of *capulanas*. It is her that I credit with my first tasting of frog legs, in the

1

creamiest soup one could ever have sampled, and my first chew of the famous ocean-side *batatas fritas* and *camarao* as well as my elder sister's first cornrows. I could go on and on about my mother and her groupies but the point is this: she was vivacious and loved life! But she was methodical and cerebral in her doings, always admonishing us, always reminding us that everything must be in balance, that you can do everything and anything but that moderation is key. So yes, My mother drank a little, and danced, a little. She laughed, a little. And had some infrequent times of heavy, pensive moments whilst sank deep in her favourite couch in the living room. She enjoyed a little bit of cheddar cheese, cucumbers, and tomatoes and sipped occasionally on her red wine, beer or gin and tonic. I think it's where I get my "everything in moderation" life slogan. My mother's first name was Verity and we all got to know her as the soothsayer cause she was the truth. She never did anything lightly, so best believe if she was getting us and her groupies on a road-trip from Maputo to South Africa that she had done her fair share of research and pre-planning, because here we were late that morning all bundled up in the minivan, sipping on Sparletta cream-sodas, playing card games and listening to the radio at real loud volumes and not caring what else was going on.

As we approached what appeared to be our first road block of sorts, my mother signalled to my sister seated at the back, asking her to bring forward a bag she had stashed behind a seat. It contained several cans of *cerveja*. When we were stopped we all quickly established that this was the sort of operational border at that time. No set office, no flags. Just a barricade made up of several bricks and non-smiling soldiers, the uniform of which we could not clearly identify. Were these friends or foe? Mom's Mozambican friend conversed with the soldiers. A few minutes later the cans of beer were tossed their way and our minivan was let to cross that border and roll off into the thousands of miles of no-man's land ahead. As our driver then pushed the accelerator harder we all let out sighs of relief. Someone mumbled some silly joke and we all relaxed into laughter. We had just passed our first roadblock ever and that was possibly my first memory ever of interacting with authority figures. Lesson learned: give them what they want and all will be well. I knew my mother had planned ahead. She always did. There was a safety and an ease with doing things with her, and I believe this is the first counsel I ever got through life from my mother: be prepared.

2

You are capable. Don't think you are not. But don't ever be ill-prepared. Plan ahead and all will be well. She and her lady friends had prepared enough to make that early childhood experience of mine memorable. They took turns at the wheel, the others huddling around the driver, sharing all kinds of funny stories from days past and laughing without a care in the world. It was a memorable trip for so many reasons-among them, possibly, my first burger at a Wendy's, my first huge box of candy- a set of 12 tiny Smarties, that I absolutely didn't like any more, but had bought to dig inside for Barbie doll coupons-there were giveaways, a lucky girl could win a barbie, and at the time all my girlfriends at the international school were into those. After the colourful shopping, lots of fast food and way too many carbonated canned drinks we made our way back to Maputo. Again, my mother remembered her stash of cold *cerveja* for the "border guys" as she called them, this time packing tins of Lager beer into a bag and stuffing it with serviettes at the top. I do not recall whether it was the same team of scruffy bearded soldiers that met us on our return, but the beer was gifted at some point and we all got safely home. It was when we got settled back home that evening and turned on the tv that the shocking, yet thrilling realization of what we had just done fully registered to me. We had just done a long cross-border return trip across land in which a full scale war was ongoing. four women, and their kids tagging along, mostly pre-teen girls. As I saw gun-powdered and bombed-up images on the local evening TV news I thought to myself: my mother is a hero!

We had been living in Maputo then for over 3 years at this time. My mom had been a young, rising professional in the Ministry of Trade back in our country. Her reward from the government and country she served came in the form of an appointment to serve in the Foreign Service as an officer at the Malawi Embassy in Maputo. She jumped at the chance! My father was a fully-employed accountant and opted to stay back home in Lilongwe. My late father passed away when I was 9 years old, hence my many more memories of life with my charismatic mother, and almost none of him. Mom kept the house spick and span, doing what little domestic chores she could here and there over the weekend. For the week we had a fantastic househelp known as Laurinda, a Xangani woman that taught me how to make soup from scratch and bake perfect coconut sponge cakes in baking tins made of mozambican aluminium. Laurinda was a wife and mother and walked to our home to work every morning and returned home each evening after six. In the time we had her I watched her carry and birth three children, so half the time she was pregnant! She was a beautiful, resourceful and kind-hearted woman who got to know more about my mother's house than mom did, for which we were grateful.

It's to her credit that now I am a baker and have some domestic bone in my body. She taught my sisters and I how to shell Mozambican prawns, how to pick out a decent aluminium cake tin at the local market and how to keep a household afloat with no running water for weeks on end (we had two huge drums to store water in on our twelfth floor balcony during our entire stay in Maputo. On occasion there would be no running tap water for up to two weeks). She was also instrumental in getting me started on the onslaught of hairstyles that I've had over the years as when I was nine she took me to her friends for my first time ever box braids. Wish I had a picture of those; the search continues! Laurinda was the first "employee" my mother had that I saw in uniform, and she was proud of that blue, pink or striped kit! She would show up to the flat by sunrise, go into the bathroom and emerge with a well-ironed uniform each morning, work all day in it, then return it to the pantry closet by sunset each day, ironed and folded where necessary. I witnessed her growing belly, then cradled her beautiful children that she lovingly brought into this world. Each time, shortly after she gave birth, without excuses and without asking my mom for extra time, she would be back at our flat: cooking, cleaning, mixing, serving. And always, with a smile. Her strength and femininity inspired me. Would I turn out to be as stoic a woman as she? Her physique is etched to my memory not only because she was one of my earliest nannies, but also because in 1987, when I was seven years old and we were living on the eighth floor in that apartment, known as the *trinta e três andares,* we were locked up together in our bathroom one unfortunate midday: she, my elder sister, Grace and I. I tell this story often because it was the first time in my life that I learned what grave danger meant, felt vulnerable and saw how others were available and even eager to take away what others had. It was a new and foreign concept to me. The ongoing war, poverty, and economic gaps in Maputo and the whole country at the time gave rise to many pockets of thievery and other forms of criminality. My mother, being a conspicuous embassy employee and a single mother was possibly profiled and seen to be an easy target. The bandits must have been watching us and knew our schedules when one of them courageously showed up at our front door. Well, he must at least have known about our water problem (that week we had no running water in our bathtub taps, and had requested a plumber at a local company). He rang our doorbell and Laurinda answered the door. It was just before lunchtime on a friday. Normally my sister and I were picked up by our driver about an hour or two later as we had afternoon classes that week, and usually set off for school shortly after lunch. Well, on this day we all raced to the door. Laurinda competently dealt with the guy in perfect Xangani then we all headed for the bathroom, as the guy appeared to be a plumber, eager to get on with this work of drilling and fixing things in there, *"as the reports said"*, he offered us. Like sheep about to be slaughtered we led the way to the bathroom, me in front of the pack, then Grace, Laurinda behind us and the bandit guy trailing behind. We all wanted to share which part of the taps we had most problems with. As soon as our eager heads and legs stepped past the bathroom door, the guy pushed all three of us in as forcefully as he could and then proceeded to shut and lock the door to the bathroom. Inside the bathroom, we all landed somewhere on the floor- my sister and I using our hands to hold Laurinda from falling flat on her tummy and heaving her up where needed as she was heavily pregnant at the time. We could hear his outside movements-frantic, panicky and disorganized. It appeared he had removed the bathroom door key from its place and was running out towards the front door, possibly with it in hand. Or, it was possibly his pocket because at some point we heard it clickety-clack down to the ground. *Idiot!* Then, in a second faux-pas the bandit rushed out our front door and we heard his footsteps as he rushed down the stairs. He possibly had buddies down there or outside to bring in. His one error? In this haste the wind slammed our front door tightly shut behind him, barring him from re-entry as it was the sort of old oakwood doors that required a key each time and had a magnetic effect upon closure. Soon enough we learned that in fact he really did have some burglar mates outside who were ready to get in to grab most, if not all of our property, and an empty truck was stationed outside, awaiting loading downstairs on one of Maputo's main streets. Laurinda had her ears pressed to the door, listening in to their muffled conversations from outside our front door, and occasionally she was translating for us. *Idiots!* After some time of loud arguing and their loud attempts at breaking our door down, to no avail, we heard the last of them scamper down the twelve flights of stairs of the building. Inside the bathroom we had worked out a plan of how to get out. There was a small piece of glass above the bathroom door. We agreed that if we broke it using some heavy bathroom bottles one of us could climb out, track down the key outside, call the police/mom and then open for everyone else. Grace was the most agile, so Laurinda and I put our hands in position and helped her up to the above-door level (she had one of her legs parked on the bathroom counter and one on our joined hands). She managed to get out, found the key with little difficulty and let us out. We were all sweaty, hot, hungry and tired, but we grouped hugged-it out before we proceeded to call mom at her job on the house-phone (thinking back, how nice a cell phone and whatsapp connection could have been on that day. I digress...). Before she even picked up we heard a loud banging on the door and at the exact same moment the doorbell rang. In shock, the three of us just cozied up together, afraid of what or who may be out there. Could it be one of those idiotic goons again? A minute of silence, only our heavy breathing, followed by the loud voice of our driver: *"It's me. Open up!"*.

Was he one of them? Laurinda asked him in Xangani.

"Of course not. Am here to pick up the girls."

Laurinda slowly opened the door to him, one millisecond at a time, each time pressing her face to the door, scoping out the territory. He had come early to pick us up for school, waited and got frustrated when he heard of the bandits' scheme as several homes had already been raided at this point in the neighbourhood. We spoke to mom, who was relieved we had made it through the saga safely and could make it to class on time. Yup. We made it to school after a 30 minute lock-up and a near-theft in our own home. Imagine the stories we had that day on campus! In hindsight it has always served as my reference point for when I've felt and feel unsafe, invaded or overwhelmed. Funnily, this experience is an ideal glimpse of what it's like to live with HIV or to feel vulnerable or be taken advantage of by another in my view: stupid and as if you didn't do all you could. When, in fact, the truth is, you probably did the best you could with what you had/knew at the time and how could you have known any better? It's one of those things where you are just wiser after the fact than before, and sadly, you can't "turn back time" as there were so many factors other than your disposition to the equation.

What I know of fashion and fine dining etiquette, I learned from my mother. She wasn't at all times a flashy dresser, preferring a more varied closet. But when she was honoured with an invitation to dinner, to a function, to drinks, she sure knew how to glam herself up. I'd be the lovestruck kid smiling by her bedroom door when she prepared before an outing. On many occasions I got to share in her lipstick joy on my cheeks or to shake and spray her perfume into her hair, neck and armpits. When the occasion was an Embassy event at times we would together with my sisters turn this time into an elaborate family occasion- handing each other her various colourful clothes from the vintage suitcases that she kept under lock and key in the wardrobe that faced her bed in her room. Mom would indulge us, trying on each three piece attire and modelling it out for us from her bathroom into the room as we cheered on and clapped gleefully. One she wore often was a reddish one that had images of the black chicken on it. I came to learn later this was the party cloth of the party in power at the time[3]. She looked queenly and fierce each time she wore one of those outfits to an important function. In fact, I was always enamored by my mother, mostly for this quality in her that I couldn't quite put into words: an ability to be both hard and soft at the same time. I remember growing up feeling like if I could just turn out to be half the woman that she was that I would be alright in this world.

When we lived in Lusaka, Zambia there was a period in which petty crimes were on the rise. Most houses, expat communities and offices were robbed, mostly at night, but at times in broad daylight. A majority of the time news reports shared on the local television station, ZNBC, indicated that most of these were an "inside job", involving the domestic servants, security guards or others with rights to be on the premises. Our residential compound, owned and managed by the Kenyan Airways at that time, in Kabulonga, about a 2km walk from the famous Melissa supermarket, was no exception to this occurrence. Housing various expat families: the elderly

---

[3] MCP, The Malawi Congress Party ruled Malawi from 1964 to 1994 in a one-party state until a referendum was called on by the country founder, the late Ngwazi Dr.H. Kamuzu Banda.

dutch couple that played tennis a whole lot (IMO!) in House number 1, the Zimbabwean single-parent-headed household run by mom's friend from the Zimbabwean High Commission in House number 2; our family in house number 3; the Kenyan family with links to the building owners in House number 4; and the intriguing Ethiopian Family in House number 5 headed by a UNICEF director...all of us at some point in time in one year got a taste of this robbery. On one occasion we woke up in the wee hours of the morning to find the thieves had taken nothing but clothes left out on the clothing line, including my sisters two pairs of underwear and one side of my bathroom slippers. Side-eye! What ridiculousness! Who were these people? And so it was that my mother and two of her sister-friends in the neighbourhood bought guns. Not the quiet, cute, small pistol-type guns. The AK47 type of guns. That they kept in the house! Mom kept hers in the top shelf of her wardrobe, right next to that vintage suitcase. The gun was always firmly, securely in its bag, laid flat, as opposed to upwards, as it wouldn't fit in there otherwise. Every fortnight or so, or post-robbery, she and her buddies would gather around at the back of our house and shoot loud shots from their guns into the air. I know most of the bullet shells fell into the empty field that was behind the wall of our Kabulonga neighbourhood compound. Because behind our building was this huge stretch of empty land that laid bare for the longest time. The thieves, working alone or in groups, were once in a while caught running through this ground to nothingness or the stretch of forest that existed between the area known as Kabulonga and Ibex Hill, an area west of the rich Woodlands area, that was also a hugely targeted residential zone at the time. Once the families made the shooting a practice and once a neighbourhood watch committee was set up eventually the robbery rates started to go down. In the process many of our security guards were caught as having been accomplices to some very crafty and creative neighbourhood robberies. On one instance, for example, when the Ethiopian family had left and been replaced by a Tanzanian one a group of nonsensical thieves broke in one night and not only did they steal some household items, they treated themselves at the family's readily-set dining table to a fancy dinner that had been pre-cooked by the maid earlier in the day and left dirty dishes in the sink on a friday night. Crazy. But my mom? Fearless! She and her buddies continued to shoot into the darkness of the nights whenever they could after that incident.

When we moved back to Malawi in the late 90s and she agreed to take a job in the Vice President's office I saw more of mom as a peacekeeper. She was in love with her family, and all the dynamics of her brothers and sisters at our village in Ntcheu. She wasted little time in getting involved so soon enough our home in Lilongwe began to fill up with a lot of out-of-town visitors most of the time- some family, many friends, a lot of new acquaintances. Mom was a bridge-builder. We travelled often to our village home in Ntcheu too: Zalengera village, T/A Ganya, Ntcheu Boma. This is a place I can get to in my sleep. Many laugh when I say I am a *"Mhango, from Ntcheu"*, for the Mhango name is so northern a name in malawi. Around this time I was enrolled in Lilongwe private School. I was a student and soon became a prefect and later head girl in this predominantly Indian school with few locals in attendance. This made me stand out. All of us local students did. By that of course I mean black, for the Indians were also local, but most had a second passport to elsewhere, and more life options than we did. Funny thing is all of us that were black in my class all graduated with enough points to make it to the local University whilst most of the Indian girls got marriage proposals or got to help run their family businesses, like the case of the boys. What? Marriage? My friends and I would chuckle all the way home, *"we're too young for that!" "we've got a long way to go before that, geez!"* and so it was that I set off to Chancellor College in Zomba in early 1998. There was no but, what if or are you sure about this in our perception of things. In the late 90s, any girl who was a Malawian educated schoolgirl knew that school, good grades and degrees came first, then the husband and kids, if they did at all. We were offspring of proud women who had benefited from education investments in the late 60s and our mission was simply to go beyond our mothers' achievements in life. At least I did. I had no doubt in my mind about what I was going to pursue at that point. My dream then was to become a lawyer. Just like my *Shero,* Dr. Hawa Sinare, another of my mom's fiery and phenomenal friends.

Doctor Hawa was a sophisticated Tanzanian woman, and once she moved into our old neighbourhood in Lusaka she and my mom became fast friends. She and her family moved into house number 5 in our compound in Lusaka (moved in after the Ethiopian family) after years of living in

Europe. I learned later that she had been a senior legal counsel at the PTA; the Preferential Trade Area, one of Africa's leading subregional economic cooperation arrangements and organizations. In my eleven yea-old eyes, *she was fly.* She's the first black, african woman that I saw as self-made - because she drove an E-Class Mercedes-Benz in the fierce gold color and when she drove she had a different pair of shoes so she would be wearing flats when driving but the minute she got home and she was stepping out of the car she would step out in these five or six inch, glossy stilettos that just screamed class. On many occasions I would be at our house window maybe by the living room drawing the curtains or something when I would see her car come through and as she drove into her garage I would watch this performance unfold. Pure elegance! And, she rocked the shortest, cutest afro to boot. I fell in love with her and got a bit obsessed with her lifestyle. The closer her relationship with my mom got, the more I became like a spy of her world, and so would tag along or invite myself to her place. It wasn't too difficult at times as she had a niece named Mwasi who was about my age that I could play with. I wanted to know everything about her: who was she? what had she studied? How had she earned her way up to Germany and the PTA? How could I become her? I learned soon enough that she was a lawyer and that was it-goodbye to "I'm going to be a flight attendant" and "goodbye I'm going to be the first blackafrican woman who becomes an astronaut" and goodbye "I'm not sure what I want to become when I grow up". I now knew she was out there doing something significant and wanting to change the world so would I. I knew that I wanted to make a difference on the planet and saw it in big bold letters: becoming a lawyer that was the way to do that. I would become a lawyer; make good money, live well, but also make a huge difference in the world and for my people (hadn't as yet defined who my people were at the time though). At the time as a student at the American Embassy School in Zambia I had been introduced to so many career options. One of my favourite teachers, Mr. Robert Fairfield, was very passionate about physics and space and he would occasionally show us NASA videos and talk about the wonders of outer space. I got into it so much too that one time I bought a telescope and considered one day becoming an astronaut. But overtime reality sunk in and I realized that could have perhaps only happened if I were American, or had better grades but my grades in physics at that point really sucked. At some point in social studies class, a bit of history and geography and the plight of our people as Africans started to appeal to me as development challenges were outlined. There too was a bigger end goal of doing something for the people that seemed honourable and needed but also perhaps what was more possible: development work. So, I gravitated towards the social sciences and studies, watched more and more of CNN and BBC and learned lots about Boutros Boutros Ghali and all the scary images of war in the 90s in many african states. To do something about our development, to make a change somehow, that was the goal. Becoming a lawyer was step one toward this dream and I had a full blooded, living human woman as proof that it was attainable.

We had been so sure of my passing with flying colours to make it into law school that over the break as we awaited the college acceptance announcement my mother had arranged with some of her old friends an internship with a local law firm. At the ripe old age of 18 and 19, then, I was so focused and supported that I was privileged to get the chance to be an apprentice at Chizumila and Company, based in Lilongwe. It was just an attempt to give me a sense of what life would be like as a lawyer. Mrs. Chizumila had been a friend of my moms and gladly accepted to mentor and coach me. Honestly? Tried as I might I did not enjoy reading lengthy judgements and heavy law books, though on occasion could stumble upon the odd funny, odd or very peculiar cases that proved to be light reading. Khumbo, another intern, and I had to show up for work dressed in non-bright (dull), non-glittery outfits and speak in what we then joked was *"Legalease"*. But, what I did seem to enjoy and picked up from my limited time at this firm were the drafting of affidavits, visits to prisons, interviews with people, now classified as criminals, who had been wrongly-imprisoned or locked up without trial or even formally known charges. They were unfairly forgotten in the justice system. One case I remember is of a young man we interviewed that had stolen about four chickens a neighboring farm. At the time we were questioning him, at one of the worst penitentiaries I have ever seen in my life, he had been at this facility for well over forty-eight months and clearly had some skin disease going on. His case had never been brought to court and here he was languishing in a prison cell, working hard all day to break pieces of rocks and dying a silent death inside. I felt for him. I did what I could during that time of work and happy to say we managed to present a few such cases on remand to quick trials, and few such "wrongful prisoners' were released. This entire grueling process of many visits to prisons, sitting through court processes-with the magistrates wearing white wigs atop their heads, in either of the three most formal skirts I owned at the time, was a very educational and motivational experience. One day I said to Khumbo that I was *"unquenchably in love with the law"*! Yes, I would become a lawyer, save some people from wrongful imprisonment and protect human rights! It solidified in me. I had found my "people". My people were people that were vulnerable and marginalized, people that didn't have their own voice. Choosing to be a voice for the voiceless was the clairity I got before starting college.

Well, by January of the following year I was on the way toward that dream: a first year college student at Chancellor College, the largest campus of the University of Malawi, based in Zomba, Malawi. I had been accepted to study PAS: Political and Administrative Studies, and I saw this as my ticket into the Law School the following year, depending on my grades. I never saw grades as an issue before, but got a rude awakening into tertiary level demands when my final grade was deficient by a few percentages to make the Law School entry level. Shocked and personally ashamed I pushed on, pushing to get the next best thing: a top tier first degree with hopes of trying again following graduation. I did. In that second year of college time I remember my mother came to visit. She was strong, proud and applauded all my efforts that far, never once letting on that she was sick. We took a walk, I showed her around the chancellor college campus, introduced her to a few friends. I found out a few weeks later from my elder sister that mom at the time had recently been diagnosed with a tough illness and was no longer at work and in her home in Lilongwe, but staying with her in Blantyre and undergoing treatments at the famous Mwaiwathu hospital.

I had planned to see my mother on the first weekend home on a college break as we as a family heard she was progressing well at the hospital. I took a coachline bus to Blantyre. Instead of a normal welcome party, I was greeted by a string of aunts in *chitenjes* as I stepped off the coachline bus. My aunt Winga held me tight, embraced me and she said to my ear *"Be strong, Bhatupe. Your mom is no more."* My body quickly rejected hers-pushing her back with as much gusto as I could muster. I had seen the nervous glint of fear in her eyes when they met mine and intuitively saw what was to come and didn't like it at all. What did she mean, *"no more"...how could a person be no more?* I was a mess of tears, an embarrassing heap of brokenness as I was led through the entire mourning process. If I have survived at all, over the years I've come to know it's purely by god's grace. She succumbed to the quick, painful and merciless vice that is pancreatic cancer. Unfortunately for months, unknown to her doctors at the time her treatment was only dealing with the symptoms of her ailment. On the day before her death results of recent examinations they had conducted on her finally revealed her problem was an ill-functioning pancreas, not the stomach lining and treatment was to commence sharply at seven am. Sadly, it was a little too much information too late as earlier that morning, at about five thirty am, she gave in to death's inevitable pull. No matter what other ills I've faced in this lifetime am certain of this: there is nothing more gut wrenching than the death of one's mother. But, I've also come to know that the most empowering, life-giving thing a child can know is the first name and personality of its mother.

Chapter 2

The Crisis Years

66 **M**om, I made it through 4 years of college, and got my degree!" -Is what I would scream to my mother if she were to walk up to me right this minute. So, following on passing IGCSE exams at the private school in Lilongwe, I made it into the local university. I was selected to study a course I had indicated interest in: Public Administration. Many swore this was the easiest ticket into getting good grades and a good chance to enter into Law School, so my mom made sure I ticked it when the college enrollment forms came through in early 1997. Mind you, though we were all selected in that year it wasn't until january of 1998 that we were at last being invited to our various campuses, due to some political clashes that had ensued, leading up to college student demonstrations and the subsequent closure of the college. This, I came to learn, was a key feature of the campus I went to, Chanceller College. Chancellor college is historically renowned for being the most political of the University of Malawi campuses, obviously because it houses most of the Social Studies and law classes, as such students were very socially engaged and would *"lend their voice to political issues"* from as far back as the early protests during Kamuzu Banda days.[4] In fact, I and others of my year graduated in 2002 because of this one year wait and another six month college closure half-way through our degree programs due to political unrest. I came to learn of this political nature of campus early on, in first year, and learned quickly to stay away from "ma demo" and too much engagement

---

[4] Ngwazi Dr. H. Kamuzu Banda was Malawi's first President, from 1964 when the country was declared independence til his demise in 1999. He was a dictator who led the MCP (Malawi Congress Party) and led with an iron-fist. It took a referendum, church involvement and many exceptional votes for his presidency to be removed and for the Malawian one-party system to end in 1994, leading way to the current multi-party dispensation.

outside campus. There were also the usual financial hiccups and delays. Like many other students, I was a curious cat and had the nervous streak and the temperament in those days to get into student politics and start civic actions of my own. It took one attempted student demonstration and the sight and sniff of teargas one bright demonstration day for me to fully learn the lesson: on the frontlines of student unrest, face-to-face with local, tough policemen armed with teargas, baton sticks and glass shields is no way for a decent, young, african woman to obtain her education. It was very clear what I needed to do: keep my head buried in books, stay off drawing attention to myself and run at the sound of a rumour or ghost of unrest. The other thing I learned at Chancellor College, with much amusement, was that in first year, there was what was known as *"the April rush"* in force almost from the moment I got to campus.

1st year- April rush

The April rush was a social phenomenon that came to describe the mad dash by college guys to "name and claim" which young, naive girl coming in as a first year student they wanted. The guys would sort of select girls by beauty, appeal or charm, weeding through dormitories, visiting those they admired, hoping for their mad confessions of love (or lust) to be confirmed and reciprocated by the girl's side. Then they would brag about their subsequent conquests; at times the most narcissistic of male students publicly rattling off all of their sexual details for the entire campus to know of their mighty prowess. When I got to campus in that first year I was allocated a room with a wonderful roommate known as Christine, at the time a third year student. She brought this to my attention one night after I had naively poured out cups and cups of tea to various guys I had warmly received into our dorm, sheepishly thinking they were enamored with my brilliant mind and theories of how I intended to "change the world" once I was armed with a Law Degree. Christine said to me *"Mesho, these guys want you!"*

I gave her a dum look: *"What? What are you saying?"*, to which she retorted, *"how much tea and biscuits did you bring with you to campus? How often are you going to keep your locker stocked? I've noticed you keep entertaining some same guys over and over. Decide who you like. If you don't like them, tell them to stop coming. Here. on this campus is such a thing called the April rush; the guys are sussing you out.*" She slammed our dorm room shut on her way out to a study group meeting, leaving me dumbfounded, staring at my feet in flip flops on that quiet friday evening. I thought back to the guys I had had over. Of course! It all made sense now. It dawned on me that I had struck real enriched conversations with some, but did not particularly care for others, but had been doing the most to be a "good hostess" even when I had heard friends in other dorms were being visited by these same guys. We had to make a plan! We couldn't be victims! I had to make it clear to these guys that though I enjoyed their company I had not come to Chancellor College to find a man, get married or have his babies. In fact, at the time I had a blossoming relationship with a wonderful christian young man and leader off campus and had to make that clear: I was not available.

Unfortunately that relationship didn't work out. I buried my head in books, especially the bible which by this time I was truly, madly, deeply obsessed with. A more senior student and friend, Naomi was an amicable mentor and she and her boyfriend (now husband), had begun sharing with me various ways for me to grow further in my christian faith. Together we attended many christian gatherings on campus and prayed fervently on various occasions, for ourselves and others. Exams came then the second year of college life crashed in. The end of year exams came and my heart sank as results indicated I had missed the entry grade for the Law School entry by a few percentage points. I was livid! This is all I had known as a dream, what would I do now? Fortunately there was only one option left still open: complete my first degree and re-apply as a mature entrant into the law degree program.

"*Focus on your faith, yourself, your studies. It's all you can do now.*" Naomi quipped in often, in her soft, but firm voice.

I varied my schedule and became more of a hermit; squeezing in more times in the late afternoon and late hours of the night for library hours when others were off on break. In my spare time I found myself moving away from ultra-conservative christian groups on campus to more moderate ones. My faith was/is such that I stray away from the puritanical and strive towards more private spiritual practices, all within the confines of organized religion, of course. At this time and during those turbulent years I just wanted to believe in an omniscient, omnipotent god who treated all of us (his children) as equals. I found myself attending different services and a friend invited me once again to a Catholic mass that I had declined to go by many times before. This time I said yes. I got more involved in social clubs on campus, joining both the Choral musical group that was popularly known as CONTE and some theatre groups. Whenever there were talent shows on campus, I would sign up and show off my singing and dancing talent. It all got to be so much fun that by mid second year I was leading and choreographing moves for an all-female campus dance group that we dubbed GFJ (Girls for Jesus). In this way college was a thrill, a real social experiment, a real training ground for meeting new people, testing my leadership skills, earning the ability to mobilise.

Aside from all the exam preparations and overcoming some instances of gender insensitivities on campus there was also much fun to be had. It all started when I met this remarkable man named Cava Bhima, an Indian Malawian of notable fame. He was a bit of a character, known for hosting popular social events and as Chairman of the famous Miss Malawi Beauty Pageant. Well, at one point in my second year Mr. Bhima made a visit to our campus, and brought with him a colourful bunch of past beauty queens, one of whom was Irena Mkhwazi, a most notable beauty, and a lovely lady, one am in touch with even today. He shared plans to host the inter-university campus beauty contest and said they were scouting campuses for those *"unforgettable faces, those bouncy hips, those brilliant features"* and who would like to sign up to be tested on their catwalk? Around that time I had begun getting involved in some student politics and had considered running for the vacant position of Vice president of the Student Union. With my mother now gone and law school entry years to go I think I just subconsciously wanted something to occupy the time, other than studies. It was the fear of teargas and thoughts of random, uniformed policemen escorting me off campus that got me to reconsider involvement in the student union. I had never quite seen myself as the *"beauty queen"* type, nor ever considered modelling as even a viable career or other option. Up to that point I had lived a very cerebral existence on the planet. But as I began to mull on the possibility of catwalking to represent my campus on stage, the resolve to do it got firmed up by friends of mine who were encouraging. *"You're not super pretty, but you are easy on the eye." "Well, you're smart and at least will have an intelligent answer when it gets to that question and answer session." "It's not just*

*about natural beauty, but everything. You're ok to look at, you have a sharp mind,
you are not shy and you have some talent. Maybe you can sing or dance on stage.
That will give you an advantage."* The more I heard from friends, the more
I saw my name in headlights someday: Bhatupe Mhango, Miss Chanco.
Beauty Queen. Ha ha! The inner battle was real: should women use their
beauty to get ahead or simply focus on other strengths? Are you not being
a feminist if you use your beauty and feminine charms to get ahead? On
and on the debate still rages, worldwide. I signed up, was accepted into the
training and the contest preparations begun! A week later there I was in
a gym hall full of others eager to get ahead, to have some fun, to see their
name in lights. Around me were young women I saw as extremely beautiful,
or exotic, or interesting to look at, or possessing attention-grabbing features.
Then there were also those I considered to be bimbos, pretty-but-not-too-
beautiful, smart-but-looking-for-options or other high-falutin campus girls
who like me, had a dream that involved some chic and some glam. We
became almost like family and you know how family goes: there's that
cousin you secretly hate, the older sibling who constantly gives you tips.
Dark skinned ones and light skinned tones, natural haired ones and weaved
out heads, broad nosed ones and those with nose piercings; the lot of us were
in. We were all just looking for more things to do; entertainment; a way out
of the humdrum of simple college life.

Mr. Cava Bhima would saunter up and down, swaying his hips like a
fashion model, as we'd seen on international TV channels. There was no
one quite like him to get you hyped up about the coming Miss Chanco and
other contests. I got through the rehearsals and made it to the finals at my
campus level. Sadly, and of course, I didn't win. But a few of us who had
entered those regional beauty pageants were privileged to be invited to again
represent our campuses and ourselves in the national contest scheduled for
later that year. Yup, unassuming, not-too-pretty me made it to the Miss
Malawi Beauty Contest of 1999! Cava Bhima had guys on his team that
came to pick us up on occasion. They had minibuses, clothing and makeup.
On a few occasions we even held a rehearsal in his family home, and I recall
meeting his very supportive wife and his daughter (who helped him out with
the music and costume changes). Looking back, he really was a real champ,
giving each of us pep talks when needed and a scolding if the effort was bad.
He insisted that we get wellgroomed and have impeccable manners, like his

precious Irene Mkhwazi had. Towards the end of preparations Cava even organized radio and television interviews for each of us, and a few of us to go as a group. I remember then thinking *"this man has a vision. He is such a breath of fresh air"*. Right up to the very last time I met him, Mr. Bhima was very upright to me, and a gentleman. I saw a man who had seen an opportunity in society and set out to make the most of it. In agreeing with him I saw that we young girls needed mentoring, needed someone to believe in us, we needed missions we could be proud of and a platform in which to speak and to be heard. Funnily, this is still the case in Malawi. I still see a void and wonder how else we can support young girls. But for pageant contestants, the platform was set and things were heating up toward a december final contest.

On the final contest stage two other girls and I opted to wear a full bodied swimsuit and wrapped a silky sarong around my waist for the catwalk. Well, here we all were at last, on national TV, holding on to our modesty by covering up our most precious assets when others wore stick thin bikinis and sauntered their hips from side to side down the catwalk. Neither of us made it to the top three titles. To my relief I somehow found myself in the top five list as contestants were removed from level to level. When, ultimately the winner was announced I was standing right next to her, a few inches taller than her, in a dress that was an exact copy to hers but in a different colour. As the good sport that I was, and as we were trained, we all clapped and cheered for her. But deep down I was shattered, embarrassed, broken. I had only taken part in this contest to get back to feeling fully alive after my mother's death. I had wanted to feel young, capable and beautiful and not weighed down by the cares of this world anymore. But here was a stark reminder that I don't get whatever I dream of. In fact this act alone, of me contesting in a beauty pageant had been so uncharacteristic of me that some of my family members had called before the contest televised when they had seen my name listed in the newspapers, shouting at me, asking me to change my mind, saying such activities only "corrupt young girls' morals." Hmmm. No, I maintained. The decision to contest had been mine to take and mine alone and no, I didn't see a beauty pageant as negatively as some of them did. Could we simply agree to disagree?

In the back of the changing room when it was all done, I gathered up my things, said the usual practised goodbyes to a few of my favourite other girls and walked out into the night. I had changed from the sparkly dress I had on, but still looked pageantry in a black evening gown that I had worn earlier. I was silent on the taxi ride home. Once inside I sat out by the kitchen doorway steps and bawled my eyes out. I was done being strong. I cried for the loss. I cried for being weak and misguided. I cried for my mother. I cried for the virginity I had lost sometime months after her burial and for a time when things weren't so complicated. For, at that moment I didn't feel like myself anymore. I had always been a winner. Now here was loss, and failure and I didn't know what to do with them. I tried to pick up the pieces, mentally tracing my steps to when was the exact moment I "lost" myself, and came up short. I gazed out into the dark night and wailed like a child. I felt alone; lost. The end of teenage strife?

As the contest had taken place before the end of year college break that vacation I got busy doing an internship as a gender officer at a local NGO that I had applied to: WLSA. When college reopened the following January it was weeks since the contest. I got back to my campus routines but on my first Sunday back to the campus church choir was surprised to be banished from taking part in any public activities at oncampus fellowship. I was informed that the decision was based on my "off campus activity", specifically taking part in the Miss Malawi contest that made some of the leaders unsure as to my christian stance. I was told that these guidelines would be enforced for the next foreseeable future or until leaders saw a change. Until then I was to see myself as not being a good influence, and would not be allowed to do any tasks in front of the congregation as leaders were expected to "be exemplary." Wo! What a dent to my self-esteem. I found as time went on that several other christian gatherings had a similar stance. In no time at all, I found myself without a fellowship group on campus, alone, misunderstood and more frustrated by the growing complexities of life. That's when God sent me an angel to guide me along my path to today. My angel's name was Susan Sanson and more like anyone else Susan believed in a father that gives his children heavenly rest whilst they are on planet earth. Am certain Susan is sitting and enjoying all of god's rest right now, as she passed on several years ago. Susan was an american missionary, and wife to the Chancellor College Chaplain that came to serve our campus in my time at Chanco. I went by his office once during a particularly difficult week. He listened to me listing my list of worries and said "*My wife Susan is the one you need to be talking to. Let me connect you to her."* He got on the phone and dialled his home number. They lived off campus at a residential area in Zomba known as old Naisi where most lecturers had their homes. On a brief call with Susan he summarised my situation and asked if she would be so kind as to drive down to meet me. I'll always hold her dear in my heart and believe that Susan was a real, living angel sent to guide me during those last two years of my college life and onward toward my life as a confident young christian professional with a few skeletons, regrets and pains in my closet. Like me, Susan had been born in a christian family, but unlike mine, both her parents were dedicated church servants; her father pastoring a church, and her mother a dedicated wife and church ministry coordinator. Susan had done some exciting work in the fashion industry in her early years before eventually registering at a seminary later in life. It was there that she met her husband, the man who became our chaplain. She and I were made of similar cloth. She did not judge; she guided. With her I could be an open book. On days when I struggled with something but couldn't bring myself to say she would know. And so it was that we found ourselves in this mentor-mentee, mom-daughter, big-sister, young sis kind of relationship, depending on circumstance. Over time I learned to be more introspective, see my role in things and Susan taught me to practise self care more. At times she would invite me over to theirs for the weekend and welcome me with a bubble bath, or a special gift set by the bed, or a book or scripture reading. Her message was simple: make time for you, feed your soul with good things and you can handle whatever life throws at you. We became so devoted to each other over time and I last spoke with Susan a few months before her death. I still keep her spiritual journal, a black-covered small book she guarded closely which contains some of her deepest challenges, with corresponding scripture references to focus on. Susan would say *"life comes in seasons. There are those times when a prayer a week with food helps and then seasons when you will not make it unless you skip the food and shout out a prayer every 15 minutes."* I took this to heart. In short, whilst I had learned from Naomi how to contribute best as a christian in community, Susan taught me how to fight my own inner battles alone and in quiet prayer with God. With each step and choice I eventually found myself fellowshipping more off campus and I found a spiritual home among young Baptists and in the Baptist Churches of

Zomba and on occasion in Blantyre. I eventually got baptized somewhere down the road at CCBC in Lilongwe.

Susan wasn't the only elder christian who gave me wise counsel and follow up during those tumultuous years of college life, especially in those months following my mother's passing. I also got to lean on a fantastic Malawian Couple that were both professors on campus, some friends from the SCOM ministry, friends from groups such as Life Ministry, a campus ministry and other christians off campus such as Pastor Jeremiah Chikhwaza, and his wife (who on several occasion hosted me for weekends during emotionally challenging times) and various preachers and leaders who reached me from the pulpit, not necessarily in person. I took every lesson, every sermon, every interaction to heart and wrote down every scripture, every anecdote. For, like Susan, who had cooked for me, prayed over me, hosted me in their guest room and just plain loved me with the gift of her presence and her love, I felt like a prodigal daughter who was searching her way back to her father. My faith grew. My self-confidence returned. That determined, defiant stern look in my eye slowly returned daily to my face. By the fourth year and before graduation I felt like me again- ready to take on the world, come what may.

Old habits die hard, and I must say, a series of events started to occur that nudged me to do better. Life was still too complicated and murky for me to gather strength to do it. But early 2001 *'shit hit the fan'*, as the saying goes; and real life forced me to wake up.

The procedure

I knew I would not be keeping it the minute it was all confirmed. What?! Me? Daughter of Verity, Pregnant? at 20?! No. Something wasn't adding up. It wasn't just the fact that it was all accidental, ill-timed, intrusive, frustrating and almost choking me of any life at that time that made it absurd. It was that I knew very well in my heart that saying yes to this one thing would have, at that point, meant my saying no to everything else I had known, dreamt of, hoped for and worked hard to be. You see, at this time, over 20 years ago now, the university of Malawi system made it very clear that any college student that falls pregnant would be suspended or at least not be permitted to complete their college education on campus.

I had EVERY intention of completing my education! I had big dreams of becoming somebody and one day "saving the world". This plan, as far as I could see, left very little room for a baby, dirty diapers, sleepless nights and all else that little humans come with. My mind was made up and nothing and no one managed to get me to reverse my position. I flew to South Africa as a way of staying closer to my own identity. Because deep within me I knew that keeping that baby would have been the death of me. Still today, I am thankful for the resolve; something I obviously learned at my mother's feet. She had instilled in the young me confidence. She had taught me to listen to my own inner voice. I believe all girls and young women need this guidance very early on. It is the survival instinct we need to drill early on to get through this very patriarchal world.

The physical pain of the "procedure" was just as the nurse had described and predicted for me a week before when I had gone for a first inquiry. On my first cervical check-up the nurse stuck a huge, stiff, steel object into me as I lay on the bed, legs open wide, back down on the cold, thin, clinic mattress atop a weak bed. My entire body recoiled. "Ouch!" I screamed.

"Ehe! And?" -the nurse began her tirade. *"Is this the way? Is this how you are now? Is that how you are going to behave when you come for the procedure?"*

I looked down at my feet, in utter shock and horror at this woman's entire demeanor. Who did she think she was, to use such a tone on me? To scream and scold me like she was an aunt I loved? I had no response to such rubbish. She persisted…

"And why are you screaming, like some child?! How old did you say you are?"- I told her my age,

"Eh! We get young girls in here, who are thirteen, fifteen, way younger than you and they do not even behave this way. If you can't stay stiff and open whilst I insert this rod today, you can not come for the procedure, I tell you. Because for the procedure they use something even twice as thick as this!" She said the last part whilst holding up the metallic object and for a split second, in my mind, the whole picture of it was hilarious. I reckoned if I were half as enthusiastic about this upcoming "procedure" as she was I could get through this and stick to my life goals. I tried. I did. I can't remember much else from that day except to say when I got home I had a date and a time for my "procedure". In the days before my operation I wondered how many others like me had undergone it, and if they too had referred to it as "the procedure." The word

"procedure" made it feel more distant, more medical and necessary than to call it what it really was: a termination.

On the morning of the appointment, soon after breakfast I was handed some very strong painkillers that were used in hospitals for these types of "procedures." It was recommended to me that I give these to the medical personnel before they "start things". I did. To this date I don't know whether or not I was given it. Funnily what I have left registered to memory are the two moments- one before and one after the actual operation that I'm no good to anyone who asks me even what that whole entire saga is all about; am blank! When I walked into the theatre room I was asked to remove all my *"bottom clothing."* I stood in a corner, close enough to the big theatre bed, as if to demonstrate, *"OK, guys, am in, let's do this"*, and yet near enough the door so I could make a quick exit if anything got too ugly for my liking. I wriggled uncomfortably in my underwear. I remember the rainbow coloured cotton undies that were thin and so inadequate for this job- why had I worn this particular one that day? The ignorance of it all! *"Remove ALL of your bottom clothing. All of it!"* This order was barked at me by one of the personnel, one of two men, who were dressed in surgical clothing and were each holding a certain metal object or fixing plastic surgical gloves up their hands. My eyes grew larger, from the incredulousness of it all. I felt sick to my stomach, but then again, perhaps it was the sickness that any girl or woman feels at the heaviness of an unwanted pregnancy. I worked hard to stay awake, to not faint. My mind told me to run, but when I saw steel knives, scissors and all kinds of canister looking things laid out on a table I froze. My feet were frozen and I could not get away. The words of the disrespectful nurse kept coming back to me... *"maybe you are a small girl, then. Eh! You are not cut out for this. Then you can't go through with it."* One of the personnel set me up on the bed and told me to relax. He explained "the procedure", what he was holding in his hand and what kind of pain I would endure. Each time I looked up to him/them, he kept repeating to me *"If you hold still, there will be less pain and we'll be done in a short time. Please, just hold still."* And, each time I closed my eyes I saw the fat disrespectful nurse and heard her taunting and tormenting me until I was mentally forced to answer her back. *"Am not a small girl! I've made up my mind and am going to do this!"*

It lasted forever. I know terminology now that I wish I had no business knowing. Words like "D and C" (short for Dilation and Curettage) "suction", "kidney dish". As the medical personnel did their job, I heard what sounded like a vaper being sucked in and then out of me, almost like the whistling sound of a kettle or that of a vintage coffee machine in use. It was a horrible fifteen to thirty minutes or however long it was, cause I do not remember. To think or say that any woman or girl would wantonly opt for such a procedure is a gross misunderstanding of what takes place. It's like something you do only because a gun is pointed to your head.

I also don't remember how I got out of that theatre room or how or who dressed me but hours later I was fast asleep in the clinic bed when my friend Jane, tapped me on the shoulder. I opened my eyes and we looked at each other for a bit, a knowingness there that didn't need to be uttered. I could feel my face, feet and hands, but nothing else. Everything and everywhere else felt so cold. She asked how I was doing and I mumbled something in response, and she quickly said to dress as she had a taxi outside waiting to take us home. She didn't ask me anything else; all was known and clear: I had done what a young woman in this situation could get done, if she had access, and choice. That's when it all came back to me. Of course! I was in the clinic for…. I had had the procedure and why I was stuck in this bed. I got up to grab my pants and felt it…the most grueling back pain I had had up til that time. Oh yes, of course! The pain from the procedure must have shocked my stomach and back muscles so much that they stiffened and seemed locked in position. I couldn't feel the sickness in the tummy any more. And I also couldn't stretch, relax or straighten my back. When I looked back at the bed I saw a small circular pool of blood had formed right in the centre as I had slept.

"Here. Use this."- Jane offered, tossing me a whole pack of thick cotton wool. Not the kind you find in european pharmacies that have little cute round, square or rectangular pieces. But the ones I have only known in Africa: big transparent plastic bags of cotton wool packed together for you to go to town with, at your disposal. Those ones. I pulled out a bit of the cotton wool and as I was walking out to the bathroom to go pee I noticed the cotton had already been stuffed up in my undies, but they were too thin for the job. All the same I did the necessary second job, got dressed and got home via Taxi with Jane and slept the rest-of-the-day long.

I rested in South Africa for two more days before flying back home to my sister's home. There was no scolding, or shouting. Nor did we discuss "*the procedure*" beyond "*how are you? How was it*" *You feel fine, now?*" None. But there was an unspoken air of disappointment and expectation that lingered between us. None of us needed to say it. I could feel it. That now here I was, I had now gone and done what I wanted. Correction, what I needed. Now, it was time for me to pull my big girl panties up and do what Verity would have expected me to do: complete my education.

After a few days of rest and the end of the college break, I returned to Chancellor College campus in Zomba to continue my university degree. I graduated with a credit degree, a Bachelor of Arts Degree in Political and Administrative Studies (PAS), one of the first 3 females in this new course newly re-designed by the University, that was previously just known as Pub, short for Public Administration. In hindsight in spite of what all was occurring in my personal and dating life, I had enjoyed campus lecturers, had done my utmost to be a star student and had gleaned much from brilliant professors we had on campus like Dr. Nandini Patel (a political science expert) and Dr. Edge Kanyongolo (a Constitutional Law expert). I had been like a sponge: observing and absorbing everything and was ready to use all the newly-acquired skills in the world. When I walked across the stage, to shake hands with and receive the degree from the Former President. Dr. Bakili Muluzi, I felt relieved, as I knew Verity would have been proud. Against all odds we did this. Together. Because I believe memories of her and her wishes for me gave me strength through it all. It was a particularly amazing day for me also because at that point when I graduated I was bearing a secret that only one other person knew. You see somehow what transpired between "the procedure" and "the graduation" was "the horror" that I never thought I would recover from. And yet, here I am 18 years later to tell you this: "*I survived this. That which was meant to harm me, only made me stronger.*" It will be important for you to grab a drink now, before I tell you what happened in that time, because, sorry, but my story only got more tumultuous at this point.

 **PART 2**

Chapter 3

The Diagnosis

I made sure it was a super "out of my way" testing clinic that I visited on that memorable afternoon 18 years ago. I had had enough of the worries and the hypothesis of how things would end for me swirling in my head. Stuff like for the past two or so months I'd been having a super burning itch in my pubic area and two visits to the doctor had not led to successful results at getting rid of whatever infection was going on "down there". My doctor repeated emphatically to me that what I was now on, that he had recommended weeks before, was the strongest medication on the market that he knew of and could provide. When I showed up at his office a third time, Dr. Jones Mhango (no relation) strongly advised: *"Young lady. I don't know what you have. Whatever you have, I haven't been able to get rid of it so far so I advise you go right away and book yourself to get the following tests…"* He held up a piece of this paper with his prescription to my face. It read: *"Gonorrhea, Syphilis, HIV.*

So here I was, a week later at a famous clinic in Blantyre in the late afternoon hours. The tiny space was so crowded that one could forget anonymity. If someone knew me at the time, I bet they had already identified me and shared my name in their close networks. Thankfully, this was the year 2002, so cellphones were only a new thing at the time. After what seemed like an entire year of waiting in the tiny and crowded public space, my registered number was called and I was ushered into a counsellor's more private room by a skinny fellow in a labcoat of sorts. He looked like he had had a rough day til that moment, the wrinkly lab coat being, at this point, his only evidence of authority and strength. I nodded and followed him down a darkened corridor, passed several desperate eyeballs of fellow attendees, who, like me, were holding on to their last shred of hope and patience in this place. He knocked on a closed door, opened it slightly then summoned me in. He and a middle-aged woman exchanged some professional information, a brief chat in which I established that her name was "Chikondi", the Chichewa word for Love. This is all I have, all these years still, of the woman who I first spoke with about possibly one of the most important aspects of my life.

"Young lady…" she said, her voice kind, but firm. *"Are you alone?"* In response to my head nodding, she proceeded: *"We've run your tests. Your results are positive."*

I stared into her face, not sure of the message. Did she mean "Positive, as in nothing to worry about" or Positive, that I indeed had been infected by HIV, one of the scariest viruses and one without a cure even this far into human civilization?! My heart was racing! She noticed the panicky twitch in my eye and repeated herself, this time a little more emphatic where it mattered: *"Sorry. We're positive that you are HIV positive"*

"No! No! Noooooo!!!" I heard my voice shrilling at the same time that my heart skipped a beat. My mind could not compute what she was saying, but my ears had obviously fully comprehended what she had just said because I kept saying *"No. No. These are not my results. You will do this test again. I can't be HIV positive. I can't be. I AM NOT HIV posi…"*

At this point her hands reached out across the table separating us and held both my hands in hers. *"Young lady, am sorry. We've done your tests 3 times. Normally here, anyway, according to procedure we do the test twice. The first is the routine, then we do what we call a standard confirmation test, just in case there were any errors in the first test. In your case, because I was mindful of your answers and what you told us earlier, I just asked the lab guy to do the test again just to make sure there were no errors on our side."*

What had I told them? Oh, yeah. There had been a form to fill, in which I had indicated my age, that that I'd had two sexual partners at this point, mostly using condoms, and details about this ongoing itchiness. Did those make me more or less at risk of HIV? Chikondi indicated that even with one sexual partner one was at risk of infection if the partner was unaware of their status, had just contracted it themselves if in a committed relationship without consistent use of condoms. My heart beat faster, thinking of the poster I had once seen hanging on my college campus dispensary door. It was of a fat, pompous and promiscuous alcoholic man who in the first scene is over drinking and too handsy with the women. The caption under this drawing was: Life in the good times. To the left was a picture of what was seeming to be the same man, now skinny-as-a-rod, almost naked and with three women as corpses in coffins laid out before him. His pockets are empty and the sign says *'No money'*. At the bottom of this drawing the caption was: *Life with AIDS*. As my eyes borrowed deeply into Chikondi the counsellor's eyes, I thought to myself *"Is this what happens to me now? Do I start to get skinny and die?"* I must have said it out loud because right then Chikondi spoke to me in a reassuring, motherly voice: *"Oh no. This viral infection nowadays isn't a death sentence. There are now strong medications available to manage this infection. Mind you: they won't cure the infection, but they will help you manage. What we are seeing also is that with the right nutrition, good hygiene and a change in behaviour people are now living for a long time with this disease."*

The look on my face sought a relatable timeframe for "a long time". To which, she replied, *"Well, people are living long. You could live, say ten, or maybe even fifteen years with the right approach, good food, a good support structure, these medications…"*

My mind drifted away til her voice was simply a background noise in my ongoing mental film of blank panic, fear and disappointment. She had mentioned support. I saw myself at that moment as very much alone, my eldest sisters had gotten married a month after my mother's burial, and the other had recently moved to the US to pursue her medical studies. I could not bring myself to discuss my relational issues with any of my aunts; mostly because the closest ones were more my late mother's best friends, as opposed to real blood family members. I felt very much alone.

Her urgent tone interrupted my inner ceremony of lonesome mourning. *"Did you hear me? You must tell someone! About this. About your infection! After you leave here and, as soon as possible, tell someone about your diagnosis!"*

Her alarm buttons pushed even more alarm buttons in my head. How could I or would I tell anybody? Where would I begin?

Chikondi had a suggestion: *"The best thing we say to our clients is don't depend on others' results. Even if you were in an intimate and exclusive relationship with someone. Your diagnosis is yours alone, not theirs. We say this because here in Malawi we are seeing what we call discordant couples, where for a long time one of the couple can remain HIV negative even though their partner tested positive and they have had ongoing, unprotected sexual contact. Tell him your results are not his and he must get tested."*

At this point she found a way to get me up on my feet and slowly we walked out of her office. As we walked down the corridor to the communal reception hall I looked up at the wall clock and noticed it was well-past six p.m. and we were some of the last people to leave the premises. She walked me out the door, obviously somehow touched by my story but doing her best to remain impersonal and professional. I thanked her and was on my way, mentally going over our conversation over and over. *'Hmmm. So, 10 years…'* The results sheet I had been given, which had a big red stamp across a dark grey form was safely folded and tucked away in my jean pocket as I walked down the hill from the clinic toward the main street below to catch my bus ride home to my aunt and uncle's home in BCA. I got a scare at some point down this path as a car drove real fast past me and had to skid off the road as I too had to suddenly jump off the tarmacked road to avoid being hit. The driver hooted, and rolled down his window, screaming at me *"Hey! You! Get off the road! Roads are for cars, not people!"* The disrespect of it all! In this city this much was clear: if you had good health, a job, a house and some fancy car, you were a "somebody". If you possessed none of these things, you quite clearly had to daily remind yourself you were not a nobody. There is hardly much civility for pedestrians, geez! That near miss sprung me back into the real world, yet felt so comical to me at this point in my day and life. Here I was, now infected with an incurable virus, with no access to medication as yet, yet somehow relieved that I was not fatally hit by a speeding vehicle. The irony of life.

I walked faster to the bus stage. It was cold, and dark; dusk had set in. On the long bus ride to the street corner nearest to my relative's home I pushed back tears. I resolved to tell only those that were directly affected by all of my actions. That meant not telling the extended family I was living with, or friends I had at the time. Because, intuitively, I knew telling the truth meant, in today's language, "being cancelled". The degree I was pursuing? I would complete it. This is the one thing I knew for certain I had to do; an inner determination flaring. On the bus home and as I walked in the deeper darkness of the night, up the street to the intimidating wall fence of my current "home away from home" I got it: there was nothing much to do, but to keep doing what I had been doing all along. I would tell only those I had been involved with. Then, I would continue with my education and wait and see how long I had til death came knocking on my door. After all, a year had gone by since death had taken my mother. *Am not scared of death!* I repeated in hushed whispers to no one but myself as outside the night got darker.

Once inside the house I followed the usual routine; briskly passing through the kitchen and living room, spitting out the daily pleasantries as if it was just another ordinary day. Fortunately for me, though I was home later than usual, so were the maid and my cousins. I walked into the bedroom us girls shared (my two cousins, the maid and myself) and went straight for the dressing table stool, which I used to stand on as I reached to open the drawer above the closet where I had stored my two suitcases. I quickly pulled out my POSITIVE results sheet, folded it into as tiny a form as I could and tossed it into a corner of one of the suitcases then shut it real tight. Next, I walked into the shower and stood under it as hot then warm, then cold water trickled down on me. Over my shoulders, under my arms, across my face, around my tummy, down to my toenails the water flowed, but failed to clean up my bleeding, mourning soul. The coldness of the water jolted me back to reality and I walked out of the shower and dried myself with a towel as I stared at my reflection in the bathroom mirror. I could hear my aunt and uncle's car screeching as it did each night when they arrived and had to reverse into the parking spot. I hang onto my solitary confinement in the bathroom that I somehow now found strangely comforting. Outside were all these people I considered family. Yet here I was, for the first time in my life considering myself a poor and sad twenty one year old orphan. I had known HIV in my life at that point at least just three or four hours and already I knew I hated it. It isolated me; made me a trapped and silent observer of my own life- something new and contrary to my expressive, free spirit. I'd have to find a way to live with it. I had to. I was not ready to die.

Chapter 4

~§~ Facing Fear

A year prior to this I had been informed of the loss of one of my close friends. Connie was lovely, philosophical and poised but sadly had succumbed to an infection, passing away in her prime. What killed her was not HIV but the other deadly pandemic, Tuberculosis. I mourned her loss privately and publicly for weeks. Her death two weeks after I had visited came as no surprise to me, and yet the finality of it all was a harsh, unshakeable reality. On the day I went by their home her mother received me warmly, thanked me for coming and said *"Your friend is in the bedroom. As I said on the phone, she has been a little unwell again…"* I nodded understanding at her, and squeezed her hand for reassurance. I could tell she needed this, her statement seemed somewhat of a warning, as if to prepare me somehow. I had met Connie earlier in her illness, heard her painful coughs and so I prepared myself mentally, thinking *"Ok, it's not something to get used to, but I know how this part goes"*. I was escorted to Connie's room by a relative and I won't lie, the first thing that registered in my mind when I walked in and saw her limp figure sitting on the bed was shock. My feet slowed down. Nothing could prepare anyone for this! Sensing my hesitation Connie spoke, giving me a warm greeting,

"Hi Bhatupe. So good that you could come." The strength of her voice surprised me, revealing what a strong inner world she now cultivated, for I knew her to be a person of faith. In one of our earlier interactions she had said to me *"My dream right now is that God takes me at least into the new millennium."* Well, she had made it in! She was frail, and bed-ridden, but she was still here! Her vocal strength made it seem like the image I was seeing before me was a lie.

"Of course I had to come, Connie, to see you." I worked hard at putting enthusiasm and cheer to my words; my body inwardly shaking. I held the get-well-soon gift I had brought up to her face so she could see it, then placed it

down at the foot of her bed and was about to sit on the edge of the bed then thought better of it as my eyes darted around the room, seeking a landing place. I felt uncomfortable. What was happening? How could so much have changed in such a short time since last I had seen her? Connie must have sensed this too as slowly I saw her feeble arms tag at her sheet, bringing it up to her chin, almost as if she was hiding her face. But the impact had already been made. I'll never forget how weak and scrawny her hands were; each finger purely skeletal now, almost as if all the flesh had never been there before. The same with her face; her cheeks were gaunt and her eyes looked exhausted. It was scary, and saddening. I longed for my dear friend as I remembered her to be well again.

"*Thanks. Thank you for coming. Thank you…*" she kept repeating to me. Her voice drifted off in the room. I knew our conversation was over, but just stood there, immobilized by the horror of it all. When it appeared she had fallen asleep I walked out of her room, gave a last farewell to her mother and walked back to the bus. I wept silently on the bus, thinking, *so that is what happens when someone is infected with TB, my god!* The image of her skeletal frame on the bed refused to leave me, for weeks. It only got fainter and fainter with time, until news of her passing confirmed just how brutal and devastating such an infection could be. I always had her in mind, as she remains the first person I knew of my age group that succumbed to such a brutal infection. Naturally, after my HIV positive diagnosis I would think back to her. I knew the two are very different infections but in my mind I assumed their end would be the same. At times I would stare at my reflection in the mirror and as my throat dried up and my heart beat faster would think "*You are going to die. You're going to get skinny and die.*" All I didn't know was how long I had…, when would my wellness end and all this deteriorating begin?

It was reciting scripture that got me through such intense times. It is around this time, through prayer and spiritual support with various people of faith, including the notable Dr. Jeremiah Chikhwaza and his wife that I memorized and claimed this bible verse as my life theme: *Psalm 118:17+18.* Look it up, pray it over your problems. Repeat. It's great comfort and good medicine! In the darkness of the night or the uncertainties of the day I would claim and repeat this verse under my breath, whenever needed. I did this until, one day, I dare say, the fear of dying was gone! Beware of fear. As many wise souls have proclaimed over the years it could really stand for **False Evidence Appearing Real.**

Chapter 5

⸙ Doing it afraid

"Resist your fear. Fear will never lead you to a positive end. Go for your faith and what you believe."

- Bishop T. D. Jakes

When you live with a secret, there's no escaping it. It screams like a toddler inside you-trying to push its way out, pulling you from place to place, and emotion to emotion, wanting to wriggle out of its hidden place. That's how I felt for the first week before I disclosed my status, followed then by the next three months of silence thereafter because the first experience was not all that encouraging. But eventually the deed was done, those who needed to know got fully informed and life could go on. I had to keep things moving as now I had commenced HIV treatment and needed to be as disciplined as possible. I didn't have time for distractions: my health, my sanity, my life were now a top most priority, where I may have been less self-regarding before. Everything was now carefully measured, including my dwindling finances. I had no spare cash as I now had to save and monitor my money, to make sure I always had enough for the monthly supply of ARVs (this is prior to Global Fund and free treatment options).

Now two other people in the world knew my HIV status. This time Dr. Jones had been very clear to me: I needed to start the antiretroviral medicine right away, because with a CD4 count[5] of 288, he was unsure of whether I could wait another 3 months for further tests in order to commence treatment as at the time the WHO recommended guidelines stipulated a CD4 count of 250 or less demanded treatment. After dinner every night,

---

[5] CD4 is the type of white blood cell in the human body that plays a huge role in immunity. People living with HIV at times have low levels of CD4 cells and these are built up by the anti-retroviral medication they take.

no matter where I was my hands would dig into one of my pockets or bags in search of the medication. I had been prescribed the once a day pill. That week I introduced a solemn nightly ritual into my routine. I would crawl into bed after washing down the meds with a glass of water I had brought into the bedroom and pray

> *"God, you know what I am going through. You are the only one. Please, help me to live. I don't want to die."*

I can't claim to have heard a loud, reassuring voice. But as I watched the moonlight outside from the comfort of a quiet, comfortable room I felt a peace and said quietly to myself *"everything's going to be alright."*

The weeks and months that followed were hard. As hard as the daily Covid19 updates in 2020 are. Every day felt like a cross between a torturous emotional experience on the low end and a lively sunday morning pentecostal service on the high end. I was conflicted. I was hopeful. Then I was ashamed, then scared. I just kept my head down and went through the motions, did what I had to do, which in this case was complete my degree, as I was down to the last months of the program. Once college was done and before I would be declared a graduate at the annual, flamboyant Chancellor College ceremony, complete with the presence of the Chancellor himself I disclosed also to my eldest sister Racheal and her husband, Joseph.. Instead of judgement and condemnation and accusatory tones, I bounced into their web of compassionate care and support for my health. My brother in law, a clinical officer by profession inquired as to how I had managed treatment for myself over the past months since diagnosis. I explained how with money in my account (from my late mother's gratuity) I was able to make the monthly visits between Zomba and Blantyre to QECH[6] for the monthly supply. I shared the awkward details of standing in public lines, being "spotted" or discovered by others from the hospital lines in the centre of the city of Blantyre, or neighbouring Limbe and how annoyed I was that this was now my plight. It was a walk in the park to live with the infection after

---

[6] QECH: Queen Elizabeth Central Hospital, a government hospital with a robust HIV treatment dispensing program at this time. The policy by this time was for those infected to only get 1 month's supply of ART at a time, due to global shortages and expense.

this family disclosure. I felt lighter. The burden had been lifted! I wasn't to bear it alone anymore. Yes, of course there was still the question of how long my account could handle the monthly treatment costs at the rate they were being given; but at least, for now, I knew my family had my back. Two weeks later, I did the proud walk up the stairs of the Great Hall as it's famously called, got my degree and shared a firm handshake with one of the former Presidents of my country. It was quite the moment.

No one, but that small inner circle I had confided in knew of my status and that in itself was the biggest blessing at this time as many in the country and around the world I was hearing were being driven out of their homes, losing jobs, having their marriages end all because of a tiny virus. Photos from that day show a resolute, young woman eager to get out into the real world to make use of her hard-earned qualifications. In one, this young woman is making a relaxed, playful pose. In another she's in a group hug with fellow graduates with social science degrees. Her smile is wide, her eyes seem sincere, but I know this: inside her a dread and anxiety about the future was ever present. But she was living in the moment, being present and that's all that mattered.

Fast forward a few months later. I was not out working in the big city. I had taken the entry exams for the Law School and got called in to start classes. Seeing I was in good health, and thinking *"as long as I don't yet look like i'm dying"*, I enrolled as a mature entrant into the Law School program. I had made a clean break of all of my entanglements at this time. Those had not been many, but they had been heavy. Starting a new degree course sounded like a new lease of life. I felt like a cat on her second chance at licking the cream!

No one would know about my infection. At that time, and since the diagnosis my entire body had shut down. I refused to be held, cuddled and had a hard time sleeping at night at times. I registered absolutely no sexual desire or intimacy and no interest in much beyond fulfilling my ambitious dream. I had become like a dry fig tree; emotionally shut down. But, intellectually, I was more alive than ever. My preoccupied mind needed something else to be busy with.

I occupied myself with law school cases. Moot court trial preparations. Case law revision in the Chancellor College library. Occasionally there was group work with the few guys I hang out with, and who connected with me on an intellectual level, mostly male classmates, and a few smart, younger girls who I saw a lot of potential in. Many of these since graduated and are now fine lawyers. It was all smooth sailing until a year into the program costs for mature entrants' accommodation off campus were raised and I began questioning my entire life goals. I had always known mine was a calling to *"save the world. Do something big for humanity."* And so, why was I stuck here on a college campus, for another three years when I was presumably dying? Did a day wasted watching my limited bank account savings going down make any sense any more? The answer was no. I knew I had to start living, like, really living and making something of myself and college life wasn't it anymore.

So there it was. It happened one bright morning. That clarity like I had before "the procedure" came marching into my life. Just as lightning strikes, I felt it and was arrested by it instantly. It was time to let go of the old, embrace my fears, take a step that what lay ahead was going to be way better than what had been behind me. With renewed vigour and excitement, I drafted a letter to the Chancellor College Law Department. Something to the effect- after much thought-would like to withdraw-off to pursue some form of employment-will be back soon to complete this law degree-see you later. Nothing had been promised to me. I had no job, no "rich uncle", no plan B to fall back on. And as you know, at this point, no parents nor a family home to fall back on as in the few months following my mother's passing my eldest sister had gotten married and the other had migrated to the US for studies. I just knew what I knew: that given I may not have much longer to live I couldn't waste those next few years within the walls of classrooms and dorms, no matter how thrilling the course. Like a soothsayer who sees through the eyes and palms of others, I had slowly become an observer of my life and not a participant. What do I mean? One of the challenges I specifically remember during law school was a practice in groups of a moot court competition. My class had formed groups and I was active in one. But for the first time in my life I distinctly felt the need to step back, to support the others. I recall a smart classmate, Brian, now an impressive lawyer and artist. We had become fast friends and I saw his wit, charisma and smarts. I kept cheering him on during the group assignments. When it was time to select the group spokesperson or "Lead counsel" as the term is preferred in the legal fraternity, I fully supported him and another guy to step forward for the group. I supported, revised their work, I made recommendations for what they could say instead of what was first shared, and took group pictures. Weeks later when the assignment was done I sat alone, in my dorm, contemplating what a missed opportunity it had all been. Could it be that I had now reached a stage of sabotage? That for once in my life I had begun to fade away, to hide? You see, my normal instinct til then had always been to put myself out there, to step in the ring; to fight or exhibit. In that moment, seated by my college dorm chair by my study table, looking out I had the sudden wisdom: I was dying; but not yet dead. Perhaps subconsciously I had avoided taking forefront participation as I was afraid of the real possibility that I could perhaps not have been alive a year later when the moot court trials were taking place? It's difficult to articulate what I felt in that instance. But it was soon after that the withdrawal letter got submitted. I was dying, but not yet dead, dammit! If reading the law, a lifelong dream that I had carried within me for years wasn't giving me that buzz and sense of adventure that I needed to fully step out and feel alive, then I knew I had to go out into the world and find something else that did. Afterall, what is the difference between being alive and really living? I had to find my mojo, my new path, my juice!

It was done; I left. Two key things about my law school experience that relate to the woman I have become and what I have endured, in relation to my gender and to HIV. The first- you probably guessed. Brian was somewhat more than a fellow classmate. We bonded somehow. I referred to him for years in my head as 'my almost boyfriend', because that's what he was in essence. Brian was a loner and perhaps it was this that made me feel somewhat safe with him, as I was keeping many other guys at arm's length, nor interested in campus guys in real honesty because as a mature entrant I was older in age than most. Not that that in itself would have been an issue, but I felt like I had enough complications at that point. Brian studied with me in my dorm on occasion, we did sports together, we scheduled library hours together. I recall once being invited over to his family home during one of the vacations. Clearly, he was very interested in me, and we had a connection. But I was tense, sexually shut down and not inclined toward any romantic signs, gestures or involvement and he soon learned this. Until I left campus, Brian remained a loyal friend, one I could confide in. Naturally, he became another point of HIV disclosure for me. He too taught me a valuable lesson: that I was still loveable and had something to offer. He told me I had so much going for me and to not let this viral infection dominate my world. I held on to this whenever doubts and fears crept up thereafter.

The second is that I had started to take on more part time jobs now and as a young professional and student became more alert and was alarmed at how much power play there was between the sexes in the workplace. But a cordiality was required each time, for various reasons of social decency. In more private moments some men were persistent, leery and unabashedly desirous of "something physical", in exchange for any support they would give. Some men were wealthy and used their bank value as a measure of their success; others were simply powerful in society and flaunted that in your face at any available opportunity when you appeared vulnerable.

Nothing traumatic happened to me because I stayed clear of men, remember. Religiously. But, in light of the many stories I witnessed and heard of back in the day from women I knew, in light of the #metoo campaign, and many other recently shaped global movements and notable cases of sexual harrassment I wish to say this: the tiny, delicate details can be so subtle that even a so-called "victim" can find herself doubting whether anything grave really did happen, or if in fact it's inexcusable. I have come to suppose it is just the plight of women, or perhaps upwardly-mobile women to be so tested. This doesn't excuse bad behaviour, and I have found few successful female friends who haven't endured similar experiences. Some call it a "coming of age" trial; others a learning of new ropes. The power play between the sexes, and that of male superiors over young women certainly requires more research, litigation and our attention, worldwide. Am certain many women could be supported through such complex situations. Coincidentally, the last film I went to see at the cinema with a friend touched on the subject of sexual harassment, with the incredible set of actresses recounting many women's experience of sexual harassment in various shapes and forms in the media industry. Had not expected to, but as we watched the film on international women's day, and especially at the end as we walked home from the theatre we exchanged stories of our own "uncomfortable experiences" with men. Warm tears gently fell from my eyes and were kissed dry by the evening wind as I rubbed my runny nose with the back of my hand. Sometimes, hearing a part of your own suppressed truth on screen, in writing or through art or the life of another is extremely liberating. I remain an avid consumer of good art and a fan of most creative outlets, because not everything can be resolved through legislation, although that too is very much needed in this space worldover. What I know is I had once been pushed into a space where it was presented to me that my future would be rosy and neat if I just gave in to some sexual demands of a powerful man. That narrative is a myth. I'll always remember, and want to let all girls and young women know that we do have choices, no matter how hard it may be for us to see them at the time. We can always scream, cower, RUN!

With Law school out of the way, so too was "living with a dream in mind". The day I walked off campus was the day I accepted a new reality: there is no other fab life out there or a big goal to achieve, Bhatupe. This is it! This is life, no dress rehearsal needed. It was as if I was really seeing myself for the first time. My priorities had shifted. The secret of living with a virus made me feel like I was sitting on a timebomb. The only goal now was to survive. I had some savings handed to me by my mother, but I now needed to define what the sum total of my existence on planet earth would be about. So I took on any and every job I could get. Fortunately for me, I didn't have long to wait before what I call destiny caught up with me. Thanks to having a good first degree and some contacts in the university I quickly got myself engaged with a few lecturers who were pursuing doctoral programs and who could use the help of a research assistant or two. A senior acquaintance who set me up in this work said to me: *"don't be proud; take whatever job you are assigned. In my experience, it's in the districts that no one wants to go to where they even pay you more. If you are lucky, you'll find yourself on an EU-funded project and earn good money."* There it was. My new goal! I took each research job I could find, and on weekends would apply for all manner of full-time executive positions that I saw advertised in the local newspapers. One of the most memorable researches I worked on had to do with the link between small time vending and tax paying. In my specific role as data collector I was to interview fishermen in the fish-vending city markets in the southern region town of Mangochi district. So you know what that meant: each evening as I rode a rented bike back to the simple thatched roof motel that was 'home' for some two or three weeks I couldn't get it off of me: the smell of fish! The pay received at the end of that task made this particular job so worth it. It's also memorable to me for another reason.

On the Sunday that I left Mangochi town for my cousin's home in Zingwangwa township in Blantyre, I arrived at her home that evening to find a message had been left for me.

"Your sister called from Lilongwe. She said it was urgent and you should call back. Something about a certain Mr. Limbani or some name like that…", my cousin reported casually.

"Ah, ok, thanks." I knew what this was about. In those days of huge brick-like cellphones I owned a cell phone big enough to knock someone into a coma with one hit, haha! But it was one of those huge Nokias that took up so much money to "top up" that it was very rarely switched on. During the time I was away on research I had deliberately turned it off on occasion, to avoid unnecessary charges. I had it off also the entire bus ride as nothing irritated me more than the uncourteous habit of screaming loud into a cellphone in a public place like a minibus where everyone pretends not to, but of course they can hear, but of course they can hear all your business.

I opened my Nokia and '*flashed*' my sister's number. This is what we would do back in the day, again to save up on "talk-time". If it wasn't a big or new thing and the person was expecting your response, by flashing you indicate your availability to talk now and they would call you back. True to form, in less than five minutes, Racheal called back. Our conversation was short and sweet.

"Yes, that man, Mr. Lembani, from that office you wanted to work at. Remember him? Well, he called. Said it's urgent and that you should call him back. He said something about being in Blantyre and that you should not delay. Do you have a pen and paper with you? Here's the number…"

As I took the number down I felt my heart racing faster and faster. I hadn't yet unpacked my things from the bags I had taken with me to Mangochi, but I knew I had to attend to this immediately. As my cell was low on talktime the only available option for me to have a proper call with this man was to go by the corner store and computer cafe before they closed, and they closed at about 8 pm. I grabbed some cash, put on my shoes again and walked down there. It was a cool, dark evening. Inside the computer cafe, I paid the needed deposit and was assigned a cabin number. I dialled Mr. Lembani's cellphone and after 3 rings he picked up at the other end of the line and I said, quickly,

"*Hello, it's me, Bhatupe. I am responding to your message sent to my sister. Please call me back on this number.*"

When he acknowledged my notice I hung up the phone and waited for his call.

"*Miss Mhango. We had your number on file, from about a year ago when you made a visit to our office in Lilongwe. At the time we had no openings, but I am delighted to let you know of a vacancy we have at present, and one that we are already actively recruiting for. It's why I am in fact here in Blantyre for this week. My boss has put your CV down in the shortlisted pile, and am calling to find out if you are still interested in interviewing for a position?*"

"*Oh, ok. And, what position would that be for?*" my heart was beating faster.

"*The position of Program Officer.*"

"*Oh yes! Yes, of course! Am still interested in interviewing, how does that go, am in Blantyre at the moment…*"

"*So am I. So are we. So, my boss, the Regional Manager for KAF, Dr. Margraf, based in our regional office in Maputo, Mozambique is in the country and we are on this recruitment exercise together with a certain consultant…*"

He went on and on, explaining their week's plan, their philosophy, their ideal candidate. As he spoke I recalled my visit to their office of the year before. I had seen their program on the television one night whilst living at my sister's and inquired as to whether she had heard of them and their work, a lot of interesting work in democratization and training of politicians. From the program on TV, I had gathered that they were German-funded or were an international organization with some German ties, but knew little else beyond that I saw quality, hope and a future in their work. That night I had said to my sister: "*There. That's where I want to work. That's the kind of work I want to do. Work that uplifts people. It's politics, but it's not dirty politics, you know…*" Rachel had nodded her agreement.

"*Yeah, I know what you mean. Their logo looks familiar, but I don't think I know where in Lilongwe they are at. I'll ask around at the office.*" At the time my sister worked at ESCOM, the electricity supply company and she had many contacts in her day. It took about two weeks from the day we saw the KAF logo on a TV program to the day she said to me one day on her return from work, "*I've found it, Bhatupe! That KAF place, the NGO we saw on TV. I have their address, I know where they are!*"

My sister is an accountant and part of her duties included a weekly drop in at a certain bank. Turns out the bank she frequented was right around the corner from KAF offices. One day on her routine schedules, she looked up and there was their logo on a huge sign smiling back at her. Serendipity! I wasted no time. I didn't know how these things worked, but I had a mind to get noticed at this grand office. The very next day I made my way to the KAF office reception soon after lunch. This is the day when I deposited my CV with the receptionist after a brief few minutes with their Country Coordinator. I had just walked over, really, and introduced myself. I explained to him how I had been captivated by the television program where their work was highlighted and resolved to find their office, and here I was, ready to work. Well, I really didn't know how it worked. At that point I had done college vacation interning as a gender officer at a women's rights ngo, had worked prior to this at an estate agency (a gig arranged by my older sister) and interned with a lawyer (a gig arranged by my mother). Unfortunately my enthusiasm was curtailed by his firmness: they were a small office, with a small budget and at present no vacancies were in sight. He would keep my cv on file and alert me should anything suitable open up. He noted my credit political science degree and circled it on the paper; said this was ideal. I said goodbye to him and his bright-faced, cheery receptionist shortly thereafter, feeling a slight tightness in my throat that hadn't been there before. Funny, I hadn't contemplated this possibility. I was so naive in my quest for a job that I had believed my CV spoke for itself and I would be seen as a natural fit for their organization and be hired on the spot. As I walked down the two flights of stairs from the office to the road reality hit me: I was someone who jumped into situations and thought thereafter. I needed to do a better job to avoid hurting myself. Bummer. It sucked to be rejected when somehow I had felt with every ounce of me that I would work at this place. A year later, here I was on a Sunday evening speaking with Mr. Lembani on the phone. I interviewed that week, got the job, and as the saying goes, "the rest is history". Once again, my instinct had been right. I would follow this inner voice to the end of time.

Chapter 6

Big dreams, Huge Hopes, Bigger Bosses

"Without a dream, you'll not get anywhere."
-Kofi Annan, Former UN Secretary General

On my first day of work at KAF is when I found myself deep down in waters that I had never swam in before, but got positively giddy at the challenge. I felt alive! As agreed to on a call the previous Friday when I agreed to take on the job I arrived at the office at eight am sharp, in time to see my terms of reference and sign my contract. Except when I got to the office, all was in order but none of my superiors were there. I walked into the reception to find the same bright-faced lady I had once met before, Chakupa at her desk, with some papers for me to review. The first sheet of paper asked me to draft my own TORs for the job I had just landed. What?! Some of the things we agree to in life, yikes! In hindsight those 3 years of my life working in the governance sector of my country were professionally defining. I learned what a male-dominated world that is, I got to witness first hand political division, envy, jealousy and tactics. I also was confronted with real life chauvinistic or full-on misogynistic attitudes. In one instance I was alone in a group of seasoned male politicians who had gathered for a meeting I had set up by official letters, and funnily they presumed I was the secretary as I first set out to serve them tea and coffee in my office. As such, I adapted well- knowing when to disappear as wallpaper in a room, and when to stand out without being "threatening". I learned this lesson well: never serve tea or anything ever to an all-male grouping! My wardrobe tilted toward the darker shades of colour- lots of navy, violet, black suits-thoughts back to us teens snickering and snorting back at Mrs. Chizumila all those years back brought smiles to my face.

With the thorns came the roses: I blossomed at the annual organization trip to Maputo, Mozambique for the regional meeting and learned much as a delegation leader on trips to the organization headquarters, in Cologne, Bonn, Germany. Here I was, twenty-three and overseeing international trip logistics and setting ground rules for various political party representatives. I fell in love with my work! I picked up some German, enough to listen in to important conversations, but quickly lost it too in subsequent months. For a while, I forgot all about my HIV status; able to push this to the background of things; I never brought it up. I attended church services and spoke with influential pastors who advised me *"It's not a good idea to talk about it. Nothing good can come out of that. Walk like you are healed- because you are healed; the bible says so. Don't mention this HIV again."* So, I pretended it didn't matter so much, but each month when I went down to the clinic for the monthly batch of medication I was reminded of what a serious threat to my living this "private thing was." Despite this, for the first time, in a long-time, I was happy. I was earning enough to move to my own home- first a lovely two-bedroomed stand alone house in area 15, then a flat in area 11, just behind where I had onced lived with my mother. Here I was, signing off big cheques from German donors, meeting some famous names in the corridors of power and doing my best to suppress the infection. Each time I looked in the mirror I again mentally fought back that reaction [No. I would not get skinny and die. I would live!]

It's 2004 now and I am wearing my long black pants with the long matching jacket and have a silver head wrap on, bringing a seriousness and a glow to my braided hair. I am seated between the Chief Justice and the Clerk of Parliament when I am introduced to the audience- a packed gathering of senior officials, donor organization representatives, political party heads, members of parliament and lots of journalists. Am invited to make some remarks on behalf of my organization as a key sponsor of the gathering- the Presidential Prayer Breakfast, a pre-election major highlight. I stand up from my seat and walk over to the microphone and turn to face the crowd. As I open my mouth to speak I feel seen, able and with an important voice. I've been sufficiently briefed and go ahead and convey the words of my bosses and myself for this occasion. When I get to *"Danke! Thank you very much for your attention"*, the room bursts into applause. I look across from me as I depart the stage and lock eyes straight with the esteemed member of the clergy who is also a part of the day's program and who gives a powerful prayer for peace in the country pre and post the upcoming elections. With a clear love for the country and in his impressive southern american accent, he fervently prays that our politicians would work for national development, not just party affiliation and that prosperity would dawn on all in the country, before the then May, 2004 elections. That man is Malawi's President today: Dr. Lazarus Chakwera, elected in 2020, following one of the most intriguing electoral journeys ever on the African continent, or elsewhere for that matter. I remember making my way round the room and greeting him and others that day on my way out of the carpeted, gold-tiled national assembly building. I feel both comfortable and like an imposter in this setting. For starters, it's glaringly obvious how young I am in this crowd of mighty men. I see their puzzled faces, most trying hard to place me; to see if they remember which hole I crawled out of that they knew nothing about. I say no, I didn't study in Germany, but am a local "born and bred" Malawian, a graduate of the notorious Chancellor College. I say yes, am the new face of the German INGO since my former boss recently moved to Cologne for his further studies. I say maybe, and please and thank you to any invites that come my way in all of these brief, upbeat interactions as I make my way out of the event room. Then, I pretend not to care that so few women showed up or were invited to this day of national significance. Lastly, am thinking who in their right minds decided to construct a gold-lined parliamentary building in a country so full of pockets of poverty? My mind obsesses with these thoughts as I walk over to the office's white Pajero- a staple for most NGOs at the time. I find one of my bosses waiting in there for me; he gives me a knowing nod and his face is beaming with pride. I relive that moment for the following weeks, delighted, that for once, in a long time I am not just as an hiv-positive young woman, but just a capable young woman; there's hope! I can still become what I've always wanted to become.

One sure way to forget my problems was to get involved in community work, as I have always found peace and satisfaction in being engaged. I signed up for various roles at my church, the CCBC. Through this connection I slowly committed to a village-outreach program in which some church group and partners were reaching out to vulnerable women and girls in the rural bits of Lilongwe. As I had bought my first car then- a Toyota Carina- I was often happy to drive a few women over to such programs in area 49, or area 25 or Kaoma village on saturday mornings or sunday afternoons. The women distributed clothing, taught women and villages how to farm, brought old school books for them to learn a little and then one would preach and pray for the gathering before we all set off back to the city.

On one of these visits I met a girl who sort of solidified my resolve and the inward journey I was on then. Basically she was a young girl, I reckon no more than fifteen, orphaned, pregnant and with one other little malnourished kid that she already couldn't provide for. Suddenly here was someone whose dilemma seemed even more complex and pitiful than I could fathom. An orphaned teenage girl with a malnourished kid and one more on the way in a high density village in the middle of our capital city. Without an education. Gosh! Push back tears, where to even begin waking up in the morning in her situation? In that moment, not to compare or gloat, but secretly I felt my woe-is-me attitude change to hopefulness. As we drove back into our regular city lives from the village I quietly resolved to keep that hope alive. I never spoke to the girl nor do I know her name. But for years she was my mental challenger, as when I thought of her and her dark situation, I knew I had no excuse. I had so much going for me and needed to indulge in it all. I was dying, but in the meantime, I resolved to live. Because here I was, educated, employed, and with a community and a faith. And I knew that with that faith I had the outlook and spirit to keep walking day to day and to summon up more courage and more grace along the journey. That journey has been eighteen years long and has just now led me to you.

***HIV ADVOCATE

Seasons come and go; and seasons change. In no time at all, and taking on all the valuable lessons I had learned on the job I found my career quickly changing gears as my fortune changed and in 2005, at 25 moved to join the United Nations family. All the private living with HIV, the community work and the focus on the plight of women and girls had made me see so clearly the social inequities that made a huge part of our society vulnerable to this HIV epidemic. I got very involved; spent hours at the library learning as much as I could about this virus; asked my personal doctors many questions; eventually worked my way through to the human rights aspects of this development challenge. So when one day I saw a vacancy notice advertised by UNDP for a short term position on a "pilot project', I was hooked. I applied, I interviewed, my other contract was ending anyway, so I signed on and joined this global humanitarian civil service that impresses and baffles many worldwide. To be fair it was a steep learning curve for me as having been dealing mostly with local politics, domestic affairs and here I was now, thrown into a quick moving international development field, with many moving parts. First there was the organizational jargon to decipher-ranging from agency abbreviations to positions to status of positions. Then, there were all the codes used for various programs. Then, of course were all the names of various representatives and dignitaries. I was a keen student; hungry; a sponge. I memorised everything and soon got on a first-name basis with most critical staff. As the pilot program I was on was an inter-agency funded one, it meant I had multiple interactions across agencies on a daily basis. I could be doing a staff training at FAO in the morning and that same afternoon be part of a staff meeting at UNICEF. It was a vibrant, challenging and adventurous year that I spent at the UN in Malawi office. One of the pieces of work I recall as being key was a staff video that we beamed at training programs for staff on HIV that included the UN Secretary General's One UN vision statement and several of the Heads of Agencies commenting on how their organizations were responding inwardly to this growing global phenomenon of rising HIV infection in the workplace. Through this video I first met one of the most influential scientists on the planet who also had an immense effect on me: a man known for his incredible life commitment to pursuing viruses, the Belgian epidemiologist, Dr. Peter Piot. He's renowned for having co-discovered the ebola virus and was the first Executive Director of UNAIDS, and currently serves as the Executive Director of the London School for Hygiene and Tropical Medicine in the UK[7]. I studied his face, his mannerisms, his words on screen. Before I met him, I believed him, respected him, listened to him and almost wanted to be him. But I knew my own professional limitations. From the very onset, going into the UN I knew that my strongest asset would be as a community voice, as it were, being an openly-HIV-positive woman. I was determined to be vocal and visible from the get go, because

---

[7] You can read all about Dr. Piot's fascinating life and scientific focuses in his 2012 book, a memoir, "No time to lose".

this was a clear aspect of the program I was spearheading; a sort of inner response to the virus. I figured, how best would and could the UN work as One if across agencies no one knew anybody within the organization who had tested positive for HIV, either through the very robust UN Clinic or through outside health centres? From the beginning, the workplace teams I worked with and I resolved- the best way to do away with the silence and the stigma was to find and make visible a few strong HIV positive voices. And so, I spoke. I spoke anywhere and everywhere I was able to. Soon, invitations from partner organizations began pouring in. Huge organizations, such as various Embassies began calling on the UN to share exactly what work was being done internally in its workplace response to HIV. Privately, and in many personal encounters I began to be called names. Some locals who worked at these institutions would call me a liar. Some would say, *"Look at you. You?! How can you have this disease, you don't even look sick."* I would respond, *"Precisely! That's what the virus wants you to think. That's why we have to dispel the myths about what an HIv positive person looks like and how this virus spreads."* In that year, many came to me and privately shared overwhelming stories of their own HIV diagnosis and positive lives- local staff, internationals, members of local civil society organizations, fellow church members; they were men, women, girls. I treated each with all the confidentiality and care I could muster, as only one can. These lives and interactions changed me for the better- making me a warrior, instead of a worrier. I grew strength through knowing that though there was disbelief and criticism out there that there were many whom we were representing and speaking for in these workplace programs and through changing rules, practices and laws. I stiffened up my commitment to the AIDS response and to my living. I saw myself no longer as this victim of circumstance and a broken girl waiting to find life; but instead as a purposeful missionary out to change the world. At last, who I had become, how I was living and the dream I once had in mind seemed to match up! I would wake up with a smile and think to myself at breakfast: Today, I am literally going to go out and save the world." Ego, much?! But, it's the truth. That's the rhythm and the beat that I possessed then, and this always oozed out into my work, into my interactions, into my activism.

When I worked within the confines of the UN I never saw what I did as activism, but instead labelled it as workplace response to the pandemic, as I looked at organizational policies, practices and looked into how simple, but key things such as workplace distribution of condoms and prevention materials could best be done to reduce infections. The first time I called myself an activist was following a joint event with many other local civil society activists that addressed the inequalities and limitations in the protection of human rights in workplaces and society. Specifically, this activity was jointly funded by UNDP and ActionAID, a leading NGO at the time. Working with various communities and marginalized groups, including the disabled and people living with HIV, we were able to identify key problematic issues to present at the then influential Partnership Forum, a key governance structure that reported to the then NAC[8]. At the time, former Vice President and seasoned politician, Dr. Justin Malewezi, was Chairperson of the forum (coincidentally, he was my mother's former & last boss. I knew him before and he had shown incredible kindness to my sisters and I following our mother's passing. I'll forever be grateful) But this was business! We had to barge in on his speech. Working with all local networks of people living with HIV we set up teams and decided on who would be in the frontlines. I'll never forget the bonds formed with many around this time. Getting to work with the notable Reverend Macdonald Sembereka and the flamboyant entrepreneur and owner of the printing company that printed our campaign t-shirts, Chatinkha Nkhoma, are key highlights from this time. We also had incredibly supportive mentors and key figures vouching for us, who stood to the sidelines but seemed to understand everything we were doing, people like Dr. Erasmus Morah, the then Country Director of UNAIDS, for whom, it appeared, nothing was a surprise. Dr. Morah was the voice of reason when it came to deciding how much push and pull was needed at any point in our advocacy efforts. He had a way of sizing up a room or a scenario and quietly assessing the levels of power present and needed in order to accomplish a particular task. It seemed like what was happening in Malawi then was nothing new, for many other jurisdictions had encountered such wrestling within, such push for change. The aids epidemic had unsettled many corners of society and life, but was equally offering countries an opportunity to do more, do better in

---

[8] NAC: National AIDS Commission- the local leading authority of the AIDS Response, set up in, working closely with the Ministry of Health on managing Global Fund and other resources on HIV and AIDS.

terms of their human rights records and health service delivery. We jointly as a group were just the face of it all. We took to the streets, getting off a hired minibus we had rented for the occasion when within the vicinity of the Partnership Forum event grounds. We chanted catchy slogans and made demands, our t-shirts bright and bold in concert: **"Stop Stigma! Get tested! AM HIV Positive and I know my rights!"** The euphoria and oneness was palpable as we came into contact with members of the press and they clicked their cameras and gave us thumbs up- *'for the bravery'*, they said, or *"for saying what someone needed to say"*. *"Enough Malawians have died from this epidemic, more needs to be done to protect lives, and human rights"*. We agreed, the chanting got louder as we entered our staged drama event room. *Power to the people! Hoo, hoo! Zinthu Zisinthe! We want Change*

Making the transformation to full-on *"AIDS activist mode"* had been a natural progression; a sum total of my personal and professional lives merging into a new, liberating whole. What made it even easier was a period when I found at last I had no real, human, limiting attachments. I was free, like a bird, free!

By this time I had remained for-the-most-part celibate and almost entirely free of any male touch. Believe me- there is nothing like an HIV positive diagnosis to get you seriously thinking about how to order your sex life! It was all too much at times- the pressure to disclose, the need for condoms to be present all the time, the urge to hide. It was much easier to just be a single human, living life on one's own terms. I found strength in prayer, in being alone, in pursuing my goals as much as I found major weakness and vulnerability in being alone with a man who indicated any interest. I had had a few attempts at relationships and all efforts had somewhat ended up as major failures. So I left that compartment alone.

***

I hit the ground running when I got to Geneva, Switzerland and was now registered as the UN Plus Global Coordinator, managing a pilot program that was to spearhead the entire UN system-wide internal response to HIV and AIDS alongside an existing program known as UN Cares. It was the first time the organization was shining a light on positive faces; sharing that HIV, now a global phenomenon, was affecting its workplace and that it was being a leader in this response. Upon arriving and settling into the office, alongside getting to know my impressive teammates in the Partnerships and Resource Mobilization Department I had to tick off the first thing on my to-do list: meet the man I would be reporting to: Dr. Peter Piot. Dazed, like in a dream the man I had once seen on camera in the UN documentary and talked with at a fair distance was now my boss's boss! It all felt surreal and I was pulled out of bed each morning by the rush of adrenaline at the gravity of the work, the commitment, the leadership principles the UN was seeking to share globally through our program. It made me more serious than ever: a global HIV advocate, an untiring crusader of the rights of PLHIVS, women, girls and all those downtrodden in society that rarely got to be heard, but were often listed as a statistic or a footnote. The UN Plus program was changing this way of things: both within and outside the organization.

At that first meeting with Dr. Piot- who insisted we all call him Peter - I was fully aware I was being watched, studied, analysed for any clues on what sort of person, leader I was and could be. As he was winding up another meeting when we arrived my supervisor and I waited for him in his waiting room briefly before we were summoned into his intimidating office. There was an elaborate bookshelf filled with noteworthy books, journals, magazines and what appeared to be framed pictures of some of his notable meetings, events to the right of the office. Then to the left of the office a sturdy cabinet held together and exhibited what appeared to be various memorabilia- awards, gifts and souvenir-looking items- gifted to the organization, I presumed. He exchanged pleasantries and work briefs with my supervisor then asked her to give us some time together. This meeting took place in the now-known-as "new UNAIDS building", an imposing, four story glass building that I came to learn had been recently constructed right opposite the WHO headquarters. As most staff had not yet moved in, we had taken the three to five walk down from the old UNAIDS building, part of what is still present day WCC[9] premises in the cold. It was early October, 2006- the air was crisp, the leaves were falling and I was just getting acquainted with Geneva weather.

Once alone with Dr. Piot- Peter, I saw him studying me a lot. Was I twitching too much, or projecting confidence? We had met once in Malawi

---

[9] WCC: World Council of Churches. Official website: https://www.oikoumene.org/en

at an all-staff meeting, did he remember me from then? Did he think I was headquarters material? I moved about his office, touching stuff, asking him about his travels, certain personalities. It seemed as if he didn't get this often. He sat behind his huge desk and looked at me, an amused look on his face. What? Had I crossed a line- been, perhaps too informal? Almost as if answering my silent question Dr. Piot moved from his desk office to join me closer by at the more relaxed sofa and settee that were in the centre of his office.

"You'll do just fine. Welcome to headquarters! Here's three things I will be needing from you on this job..."

Thirty minutes or so later I was again wrapping the heavy scarf I had just bought that week around my neck, and buttoning up my coat as I stepped out into the cold and walked back to my WCC building office. Brrr, baby, it was really cold out! When my supervisor asked me how it all went I reported back with a smile, *"Great; better than I expected! It's good to know clearly what he expects of us."*

I had met Dr. Piot one other time before; about three or so months following his visit to the UN Malawi country office. The former UN Secretary General, Dr. Kofi Annan had then been quite zealous about his One UN agenda and pursuant to this had earmarked the organization's AIDS response as one way in which the many agencies and programs could come together easily as one, illustrating clearly their division of labour and a common goal. And so our pilot program was invited to New York and to the UN General Assembly and we consulted, raised key points and spoke up about the links between HIV/AIDS and human rights and the rule of law[10]. Towards the end of the Summit UNAIDS convened a meeting between groups of people living with HIV and Secretary General Annan. I was in that room and met him! Firstly talks went on between participants in anticipation of his arrival and our whispering and agreeing on bullet points to raise to his office. As we wrapped up our notes a hectic delegation of UN officials, led by Dr. Piot entered the conference room. It took me a minute or two to notice Dr. Annan-a calm, composed figure; he was hidden in the line of entrants, somewhere behind Dr. Piot and another official. It was

---

[10] UN General Assembly, 6th Session, A/RES/60/1. 2005 World Summit Outcome. Resolution as found at: https://www.un.org/en/development/desa/population/ migration/generalassembly/docs/globalcompact/A_RES_60_1.pdf

when he was introduced and ushered to the very central podium to speak that I finally sensed that inward gravitational pull of excitement that gets your heart to skip a beat when something amazing happens. There he was! The man from my television screens all those years ago was right there, right here, in this room, with me, and many others of course. Or I was in the same room with this man. I took in his stature: a calm, poised, trustworthy man; he spoke eloquently and with meaning in every word. I believed him. He said he would be our greatest advocate. He said he would hear all our issues and take them forward. He said he wanted world change, beginning with the UN and we could trust him, his team and others, like Dr. Piot for strong leadership. I believed him. With each word he shared he seemed more dignified and by the end of his speech I was convinced that this was a man you would want on your team to win. To win at anything in life.

When it was our turn to respond a few selected in the room spoke and brought forward the issues we had earlier on agreed on. I spoke last; raising the issue of existing travel restrictions for plhivs in many jurisdictions as a growing human rights issue in need of reform, in light of new evidence and information on the spread of HIV. He nodded and exchanged some light chatter with the UNAIDS Executive on occasion as this went on. We felt heard. Following this session we all had a chance at a photo with Dr. Annan. I took my turn standing next to him, held his hand and smiled at the photographer as my heart beat faster. That picture sits in a frame above my desk at home and always takes me back to that moment. A moment when I felt like anything is possible. It is.

In the next two years of working at UNAIDS, with the team and reporting to Dr. Piot I was thrown into the deep end of communication. I learned to quickly get to the point, to speak in points (and to give others, especially my superiors their *"talking points"*), to write succinctly, to use UN language, and to make every single minute, hour, encounter, meeting about how to obtain our objectives. Within the organization our Program begun to get noticed: we were using all-staff town halls, the official office calendar, the noticeboards, the cafe rooms and all staff training conference rooms to bring attention to any workplace policy and issues relating to HIV, raising questions about any human resources or other standards that were in conflict with staff rights, engaging with the staff union about matters staff had complained about and even interacting with the ILO's staff association. The issues we raised were real, controversial, very private and at times difficult to tap into as they had never been looked at before. One such was the work-life balance policy. Outside the organization we supported, promoted, liaised with and uplifted the life transforming work of so many incredible organizations active in the aids response, mostly positioning ourselves with clearly activist, bold, non-apologetic voices of leaders in the PLHIV movement. In light of championing the GIPA principles[11] we aligned the core interests of the first group of openly-positive UN Staff (UN Plus) with those of bodies such as GNP+, ICW, IPPF and other similar regional groups summarized mainly into:

1. Stop stigma
2. Counter the myths around the HIV epidemic
3. Fight for the decriminalization of HIV infection
4. Advocate for the removal travel restrictions for PLHIVs in several countries
5. Champion equality for PLHIV in all spheres- from insurance packages to workplaces.

Knowing there were others who had been living and thriving with this infection gave me not only hope but also so much positive energy to consider a whole new way of living. I wasn't going to just "survive" anymore, I wanted to and was thriving. That meant getting involved, saying yes to the things I loved, experimenting more, making new friends, exploring new activities, hobbies, places. Soon, with encouragement from one of my colleagues I purchased a car and spent most weekends out at nearby towns, within Switzerland and in neighboring France. I joined various social clubs and got quite active in their planning and rollout of fun programs. There was the African women in Europe group that connected me to fabulous sisters across Europe that all had incredible stories of starting and building lives on this continent. This group gave me the Kenyan, east african and south african flair that I was missing from time to time. My most memorable activity with this group was a trip to Madrid, Spain in 2009. There was

---

[11] GIPA: The Greater Involvement of People Living with HIV and AIDS, a Principle first espoused in Denver, USA in 1983- an idea that the personal experiences of people infected with the virus should shape the response or the interventions taken.

the informal association of Malawians in Switzerland at the time now a formally registered grouping that gave me the colourful memories and nostalgia for Malawi and the occasional traditional community meals of *nsima, nkuku yo wotcha ndi masamba otendela* whenever the opportunity arose. Then there was the small, intimate, predominantly-nigerian church that I joined called RCG where services ran long like in africa, where the singing was long and loud and where the jollof rice and plantain were served on most days when there was a "family luncheon" planned. I signed up too for fun group trips and soon found the thrill of european escapades- wine tasting, cheese tasting, bread-making, chocolate factory visits, hey! Life was to be lived and I was grabbing it by the horns.

Workwise, the advocacy campaigns we conducted in partnership with many of these organizations brought about small, but meaningful changes. Soon, our program was invited and spoke at the UN General Assembly of 2007. Our push and noise on the limitations placed on PLHIVs by travel restrictions were at last met with positive responses. Changes were coming! After our interventions we were delighted to hear of the UN Secretary General's planned meeting with Heads of States whilst they were present in New York city during the General Assembly. He promised a gathering of HIV positive people that he would do his utmost to raise this issue with them, and other human rights violations affecting those affected. It was much to his credit, and to all our relief, when some countries took note of the existence of these travel restrictions in their laws. Most notable was the US one. In 2009, the newly-elected, now world-renowned, Nobel peace prize-winning, 44th President of the United States, Barack Obama announced a change in US policy and laws: a removal of an existing travel ban for HIV positive people. In his remarks, he spoke of how this continues to fuel stigma against those infected[12]. It was a major win in our book! In various small circles and groups we talked of and celebrated this major change, in anticipated hopes that many other countries would follow suit. Mind you, as I write this it exists on record that over a handful of countries still to-date restrict HIV positive people from either entering or staying long-term in their territories, to various extents. This is not right; seeing as the aids response is now in its third decade and many scientific

---

[12] As reported in New York Times article: https://www.nytimes.com/2009/10/31/us/politics/31travel.html

studies clearly indicate HIV is not often casually spread. In addition to this, the leading world body on HIV advocacy, UNAIDS now globally shares its work, indicating how to day an HIV diagnosis is no longer the death sentence it once was: "Undetectable is Untransmissable" being its catch slogan; meaning HIV-positive people on consistent treatment who maintain an undetectable suppression of the viral infection are unable to transmit it to their sexual partners, or others. Those infected can now do their utmost to ensure they do not infect their partners. Those not yet positive can make use of the now available PRep treatment, a prophylaxis notable for prevention. How wonderful that we are now at this point in the AIDS response! Eradicating HIV by 2030, as many espoused to in many earlier forums now doesn't seem like wishful thinking. It is possible; there's hope.

About a year or so later my bosses, team and I were back in New York. This time we were presenting results of a preliminary insurance policy review undertaken within the organization to this office for note and action. We were all, in fact, presently surprised to have learned that following the departure of Dr. Annan and in his ascent to the role of Secretary General the New SG, Ban-Ki-moon had chosen to keep HIV as a top priority on his agenda. So our gains with his predecessor were not lost then, and we could capitalize on the momentum we had gathered in our relationship building with his esteemed office to continue to present the voice of PLHIVs both within the organization and on occasion, the outer world. On the first day we met Secretary General Ban Ki Moon he was all the things I had not imagined him being: warm, funny and quite relaxed in approach. He introduced us all to his wife, who was beaming with joy and who agreed to take pictures with us all. We were a group of 9 UN HIV positive staff and my 2 bosses and the head of UNFPA in New York had also joined us on this occasion, as they had covered part of our team's travel costs and were a keen supporter of the now more robust UN-system wide HIV program for staff, UN Cares. The head of this program, based in New York, Laurie Newell also joined us for this auspicious occasion, as did the representative of UNFPA, Dr. Bunmi Makinwa, one of the co-sponsoring organizations. The personal stories of each of the HIV positive staff present, and those of many others we were representing who were not in the room were met with his kind compassion and sensitive ear.

What followed were incredibly professionally-enriching gatherings and periods of work with his esteemed office. That year we commemorated the World AIDS Day with many others in New York city and Secretary General Ban Ki-Moon graced this occasion and made mention in his remarks how still remarkable he found his encounter with people living with HIV. More needed to be done. We had by now visited him both with Dr. Piot, and following his departure from UNAIDS, with the new Executive Director, yet another vivacious, dynamic persona in the aids response, Dr. Michel Sidibe. The gains were not lost and we all continue to build efforts toward ensuring more visibility to the faces, issues and pain points of people living with HIV, so that solutions could be gathered and funds raised to improve their quality of life, worldover. Within the UN it was the organization's insurance policies that got much scrutiny, and in my last year I found myself responsible for this piece of work that is a harmonization of all insurance policies of this large organization. Not a light task as this demanded reviewing differences within UN agencies, programs, contract types, countries of operation, whether staff worked in capitals or in field offices, whether health insurance cards were provided or not. Indeed both the content and the process of such agreements as existed at the time required review. It was a gigantic and fascinating task. It was within that context that my last meeting with Secretary General Ban Kimoon took place, for us as a program to report back on the review work we had undertaken that entire year.

The other exciting work I got involved with was that of the Aids 2031 Young Leaders Initiative, a gathering of young minds from across the world, supported by none other than Her Royal Highness, the Crown Princess of Norway, Mette Marit. It is through this initiative that I get to know revolutionary and fabulous folk like James Chau a media star from China, Neema Ngana, an amazing Tanzanian Education pioneer, and Sara…, all who have done amazing work relating to HIV and other development areas in their respective countries and sectors. The princess is poised, elegant, compassionate, and well-spoken. I had first been introduced to her by my former boss and didn't believe her to be royalty, as she carries herself so well and is very down to earth. So, we are with her on her yacht one evening, OK, just looking around and occasionally sipping my wine and beaming across at the other participants who like me are going to pretend all the caviar around us being served and this 'Drinks after six on the boat' dress code is something we do every other day. Surreal! We had just spent the last two days hashing out all manner of social-political issues in closed up conference rooms, so I suppose a little festivity and lightness was in order now. Before this, I may add, that on another occasion for this initiative we had met at the Google headquarters in Palo Alto and been given an entire tour of this unbelievable workspace: restaurants spread out all across the premises, fridges with free drinks at all corners of the building, free laundry rooms for staff to wash clothes in at all hours of the day as they worked and of course, office designs that I had never seen nor heard of before as being A-ok for professionals. But, I digress...that was the first time we all met. On this second year of the initiative, here we were again, really working hard at solving future problems of the 21st century, and sipping wine on her royal yacht. I took tiny bites of the finger food and smiled at my newfound colleagues, the whole time inwardly screaming *somebody pinch me; how is all this even possible?!*

PART 3

Chapter 7

⚜ Ever reached a saturation point?

"When I am not joyful, I look at what happened. I don't mean joyful as in there are no challenges, problems etc., I mean when I'm not like 'Hey this is great, I'm blessed, I'm doing something I love, I'm grateful' — when I don't have that feeling, I know that I'm off; I need to course correct"

— Arianna Huffington

There were flights to and from south africa, there was signing of MOUs with various staff associations at the UNECA headquarters in Addis, there was rushing in UN cars to overtake nairobi's *matatus* and beat the traffic congestion on the way to the conference centre for an aids summit, there were presentations and online campaigns to pitch into. Then there was just more of the same, followed by fatigue. I knew it was time. I could sense it was time to give up who I had always been for who I could become. It's one of my former bosses that first presented such a realization to me. Andy Seale said to me, *"You know, some of the people you've had privilege to work with here are in this for the long haul. They contracted HIV in those early 1980s days when there was no treatment and for them the pursuit for medication is what saved them; it became their life-long new agenda. You're young. You don't have to feel tied up to just aids work* We were walking out the office building together, the one that faces the World Health Organization's glass structure and though I hadn't spent any time thinking on this point, I knew he was right. The past few years had been thrilling, empowering, life transforming even, but the adrenaline rush was waning thin and I was itching to do something new that stretched me. I had reached saturation point and was longing to pivot, change course, try something new, but what? A year prior I had enrolled in an online course with a well-established university in the UK, to pursue an online MBA. It just never quite took off as between duty travels and work demands and my perpetual interest in staying socially relevant the time needed to complete course assignments and group work was just not there. I considered committing to a full-time course, but wasn't quite sure how this could pan out, given as all through life I supported myself. Is there ever a break, a time out for a young, black, ambitious woman desirous of a brighter future? As divine providence would have it, just when I got more perplexed about this situation a crack of light appeared: a scholarship program and a university I had applied to before reached out to me via email, notifying me of their acceptance and how I had only a week to respond, either way before this would be forfeited. It was the HULT International Business School in Boston. Are you kidding me? On one cold, snowy sunday I had submitted an online application to a very random advert to this scholarship provider, completely forgotten about it and here was fate talking back at me. I instantly responded yes to the offer, but asked for further details, contemplating what kind of financial gymnastics this would entail. A short time thereafter I had an entire contract to read through and sign and all the financial requirements spelt out. The fund would cover about 65% of the tuition costs. In addition, due to time constraints the Boston campus was now full, but the school wanted me to consider either joining their London campus or their soon-to-be-opened fifth campus in San Francisco, California. California! I saw myself studying outdoors whilst basking in the sun in this sunny place (as seen in hollywood movies). The image was irresistible. Sadly, all financial calculations at the rates and conditions HULT and partners had stipulated pointed to a sad and torturous year of living. The honest truth was it did not look good. I could not afford to leave work and commit to a 100 percentage learning in San Francisco, a city possibly just as expensive as Geneva is for a student, when you include food and other living costs.

I sought advice from a few learned friends I had- both professionally and spiritually. All these friends are PhD holders and I asked them how they saw this in terms of progression in my life and career: did it make sense to leave full time employment for a year to pursue a master's degree course. We agreed that it did. That week I mulled over this decision and agonized over the financials. Angst and fear of the unknown eventually took over my life and on friday morning I drafted a sad letter to the HULT team, indicating my strong interest in the program but stating that regrettably

I could not undertake the study this year as the finances did not add up. Over the weekend I prayed over this turn out of events and sunday at church quietly asked God *"for strength to let go of that which I wanted and to move on with my life"*

The following Monday when I got to the office I opened my emails to find one very encouraging email: the board had met in an extraordinary meeting and decided to up the scholarship amount. I recalculated the amount due from me. It still looked to be a strenuous year ahead, but with enough discipline and enough focus I would just about make it through. So, not only was HULT back in the picture but I could see a short term future for myself in California, in full colour! I did the necessary, both professionally and to seal this deal, then a few weeks later I took the plunge into the world of the unknown: from full-time employee to student. I recall some of the heartfelt messages I received prior to my departure. I had met and worked with so many phenomenal people, most of whom had enriched my personal and professional life. There was nothing short of major gratitude in my heart in those days as I prepared my exit. Most memorable also is the farewell dinner some of my girlfriends planned for me. They reserved a quaint corner at the famous Phuket restaurant that's a stone throw away from the Palais des Nations UN building, right within the vicinity of the UNHCR premises. Dr. Karusa Kiragu and Eva Kiwango, both powerful, savvy, smart women, now both Country Director's of respective UNAIDS offices wined and dined me, offering me tidbits and life tips from how to survive life as a full-time student, to making the most of a stay in the US. I got home that night well-fed, gifted and celebrated. A couple of days later I was on the plane from Geneva International to San Francisco International airport via Amsterdam, ready to dare on another of my dreams, again with almost nothing and no one to fall back on. In short, once again I jumped!

***California

I landed first in a cramped up bnb in what appeared to be San Francisco's chinatown. At least this is the address my new classmate had given me via email. Prior to my trip we had been matched up and agreed to split the rental on this 1 bedroomed flat, the only one available within a good radius of our campus. I came to learn that accommodation in this city was as hard to get as in Geneva. I endured this flat and cohabiting for just under a week before settling on a bit of change; first to a student hostel where I had my own tiny room, then to a proper studio apartment in Oakland, on the outskirts of San Francisco, a city with much colour and culture. No doubt I was warned of the crime rates there, but I reckoned as a black african woman I could survive Oakland, and paid the warnings no mind. Besides, I had already made the security deposit to a wonderful concierge named Micheal. I settled in and varied my schedule daily so as to be physically safe, at times walking along the Lake Merritt side to get to my flat and at other times opting to use the backroad that led me through MaCarthur Boulevard over a small bridge and unto my street. I soon got to learn of all the useful convenient spots in my neighbourhood: there was a Kentucky Fried chicken 5 minutes away, a donut and coffee shop that stayed open 24 hours, a 7 11 nearby and a laundromat in the building. Within two weeks of trying to follow its timetable I ditched the bus, though as clearly the public transport did not have *"Swiss Efficiency"*. Other than this California turned out to be all I had anticipated it to be, and San Francisco more so. I quickly got used to taking the bart each morning from my oakland-based apartment, following a one dollar car ride between the two cities. The BART took me all the way over to First and Market and I would then walk along the length of the Embarcadero to the new, brightly-lit glass structured HULT campus that faced the Starbucks that decorated the corner.

As I had joined my class about a week late, by the time I set foot on campus the lecturers were already joining forces and getting us students involved in outdoor team activities and adventures. The winning teams won all sorts of very american prizes, including at one point a set of tickets to the Football game. I had to be reminded that this was American football and has its own set of rules. No experience, love it! Then there was what I call the most crazy thing I have done: Ziplining in some Californian forest. The school drove our new class to some forlorn zone, set us up in teams and read out the instructions. We would each be given a certain fixed time to do some on ground exercises, following which each of our teams would support each individual member to climb about 200 metres above ground on a tree, when we got to the top, someone would be there to hoist us up. Following that we were each to cross over to the other side and then climb down. First team down and reaching a marked territory was to be declared winner. *Why was I even here? This was insane! I hated climbing and thought I had a fear of heights. I would be the weakest link in my team. Why, why why???!*

My throat dried up and I swallowed and blinked hard as I supported teammates and cheered them on up the tree. The school director added one more assurance as the drills went on: getting across was optional, but each team member had to at least make it to the tree top. Finally when it was my turn, I feigned a wonder woman confidence, planning to make it only to the top of the tree before accepting defeat. I would say I gave it my best shot. Sweaty, scared and self conscious as all eyes were on me, I made it to the top and didn't for a second contemplate giving up. But when the helper hoisted me up and I was now lying face flat on the board placed at the tree top and looking down at my teammates I felt faint. *No! I couldn't, wouldn't, it was too much to ask of someone who hadn't done this before.*

"*But, this is my first time. I haven't done anything like this before!*" I shouted down to the Dean.

"*Yes, we know. Not many of you have. But that's why we are here. We are here to try out new experiences, to push ourselves further, and you all are here to learn from each other. Use your team. Get help from your team.*"

From the top of the tree, lying on my stomach, I conferred with my team, gaining tips on how to grab the rope, make the jump and get through the line. The helper re-assured me he would be there to catch me if I were to fall. Eventually, after breathing in and out several times and revisiting various flight scenarios out loud I let go. I let my feet lead me forward, lept quickly into the air, grabbed onto the two ends of the metallic gliding thing as it was pushed my way and held on for dear life as I felt my entire body careening to the other end of the forest, a length of about 300 metres. Mid flight I heard the sound of my own voice- squealing, screaming, screeching out into the green, empty woods. I looked down to face my teammates, who were clapping, cheering and following me across the zipline on foot. At descent I breathed out a sign of relief and shook my head in disbelief. I had done it! I had ziplined across a valley in California. As I faced the Dean I said it out loud: "*I did it!*"

"*Congrats, but it's no surprise. We knew you would. Look, all of you were selected to come here because we knew your potential. We knew you have what it takes.*"

Business school taught me to always remember that I was only a thirty-something year old person and had many things still to explore in life. My classmates in business school challenged me to think outside the box. Most of them were young American or Canadian white males, filled with a super confidence and stopping at nothing to attain their goals, or engineers from Asia with either tough backgrounds, strong family expectations or rich uncles and fathers willing to finance each second of their Californian experience. As with any school we had those who goofed off and those who filled up every waking moment with study. There were cliques too: the Indian one that shared naan bread or their culture at every chance, the Japanese who got top scores on each exam, and then slowly a couple of us africans started hanging out together, either to catch up on corporate finance equations, or to gossip up this, that or the other. My diplomatic shell started to fade away as the new life took more, demanded more and as life got messier. No longer the cushioned UN staff I was now the rugged student- waking up with panic at the sound of an early alarm, walking frantically to the street corner to catch my ride, then the train, whilst trying not to think about how much breakfast, lunch and subsequently dinner were burning a hole through my pockets. In time I stopped fretting and starting flying. I took on a new language, understood finance and tech jargon, familiarized myself with the best parts of the city to hang out on a dime. Life was sunny!

Towards the end of summer that year I was invited to a book launch and travelled to Cape Town, South Africa by an institute known as the Openly Positive Institute. It has now been closed down but this institute conducted a lot of advocacy and treatment support work for people living with HIV in South Africa and across the region and world. I had learned of its efforts during my UN work and stayed connected. The year prior they had invited me to contribute a chapter sharing key highlights of my life as an HIV positive african woman to a publication they had planned coming up. This was the time. So whilst some of my classmates took flights to other HULT campuses- in places as far flung and exciting as Shangai and Dubai, I was blessed to fly to Cape Town for this book launch over a break. During the couple of day's stay I reconnected with many old friends in the global HIV networks, made new friends, spoke out against barriers to quality living for PLHIVs and shared my personal experience. The organizers had taken it upon themselves to add many more meaningful activities to our stay, including a visit to the Stellenbosch Winery, where we watched a blown glass art workshop and did a whole lot of wine tasting. The book launch was successful, and following remarks from notable South African persona we all enjoyed cocktails and mingled across the room. A couple of my friends had made it to support me that night and we strolled out into the dark and found ourselves a glamorous restaurant in which to dine that night. We shared a lot more than a meal. These were my former college girlfriends and in the short time we bonded over our common experience as malawian women living in diaspora, professional challenges and all of our relationship drama. [Naomi, Sarai, I love you!]. On my return flight to San Francisco I did a whole lot of reading, not only of the newly-published book we had all worked so hard at creating, but also of newfound materials I had picked up at the airport, as I often do on these journeys. One of the articles contained a few quotable quotes and one that struck a chord with me was something about how people who have made an impact in the world were either those who were experts in an area and therefore stayed the same over time carrying on and improving their skill in a given area, or those who tried on new talents for size and changed with seasons and grew by metamorphosis. I was obviously now deep into this process of metamorphosing. Question now was What would I morph into?

Eventually I made it through that entire brutal year of study, most of us did. When I shared this amazement with the Dean at graduation he just chuckled at me, saying *"Of course you did. Remember you Ziplined across a Californian valley in your first week here?"*

Chapter 8

Chasing love

"Laughter heals all wounds, and that's one thing that everybody shares. No matter what you're going through, it makes you forget about your problems. I think the world should keep laughing."

-Kevin Hart, Comedian

I want to own up to my part in all of my life experiences. We are always wiser after the fact, not before. Especially if what we were doing was kissing a frog the entire time we thought it was a prince! Seriously, none of this is made up and I simply see them as challenges I had to face in my pursuit of love and family as an HIV positive woman. Navigating your sex life as a young HIV positive woman is possibly one of the most difficult things out there, but who talks about that?

There was firstly the "saviour". The guy who had found me at my most vulnerable, who had his own inconsistencies and deficiencies and found times of weakness in me so he could exploit me. At the time of starting a relationship with him I had my home, he was apparently just recently fired from his job (that he never had) and living with his mother. Much to my surprise and with no prior notice he slowly moved into my two bedroomed flat, first taking on the guest room, then somehow easing each night into my bed, amidst my weak protestations. We were not yet sexually involved then, but he worked his way into my psyche. In the mornings he would wake me up to early morning prayers or to the wonderful smell of a breakfast that he himself had prepared. I was smitten. How had I gotten so lucky? He continued working his magic and in no time I would give him the keys to my home and my car when needed. We were now clearly playing a game of husband and wife and he hadn't even once paid for dinner. At this point my celibacy had been a real permanent thing and when I flinched once at his touch he got curious, asked me what was wrong. I spewed out my entire life story, telling him of the infection and how I avoided men. He hugged me and kissed me on the forehead, vowing to protect me and said he was not with me for that, but for other reasons. Over time I got to know what those reasons were, namely, a roof over his head, meals and a semblance of stability. Yes he was a christian but over time I got to learn my loverboy savior had more problems than I. He had children with a woman who had taken his children away from him and was desirous of family life. In fact he was probably just using me to keep him warm, for now, until he could get to what he referred to many times over as his *"wife and kids"* though they had not actually been formally married in a court of law. He would say this to me each time we had an argument, as couples do and I threatened to throw him out, or cut his access to my car. *"Who wants to be with you anyway? You are diseased! You are a sorry *** of a woman, and who would want you anyway? You should consider yourself lucky that I am even with you. It's because am good, am a good standing christian, it's why I don't leave you. I already have kids, I don't want any with you. I stay on because who else would want you? Huh! Answer me!"*

For so long I believed his lies, not answering his redundant questions but inwardly thinking he was right and it was proven: who wanted me anyway? Truth was I hadn't been too open to exploring too much in the romantic zone. One night my "saviour" came in late, awakening the whole neighbourhood as he drove into my garage well past midnight. He got in with the spare key he now kept and woke me up. I gestured to the kitchen, indicating his food was in the microwave for him to heat up. He wanted me to rise, reheat it for him and then stand there and then sit with him and watch him eat. At nearly two oclock in the morning! I refused, but he insisted and managed to pull me out of bed and to the kitchen. As we did this I took in the strong smell of him for he was reeking of alcohol. He had been drinking again. That month he swore to me that he never touched *"the hard stuff."* Once he had his heated plate I was making my way back to bed when he pulled me from the back, tightly twisting the braided ends of the new hairstyle I had just got done that week. Ouch! He yanked me toward the front and my head hit the end of the kitchen doorway, my forehead bumping into the top part of the wall above the stove. I was now fully awake and would not take this, what I considered domestic violence, lying down.

But looking at the time I reckoned it was unsafe to do anything about this at three am. I went to bed. He sat in a hot bath for hours then came to bed and tried touching me around. I played along. In the morning dressed for work and after breakfast I gathered all his things and put them in a plastic bag. I confiscated my house and car keys, woke him up and said this:

"*Listen. I've had enough of you. I am going to work now. When I come back this evening I don't want to see you or your things. All your stuff is in a bag. I don't want to see it either. Have a great life.*"

He just blinked back at me, a blank expression on his face. Sure enough, that night he was gone. But his stuff was still there. I found a way in the days after to get it all safely to him, communicating in a zig zag way to those we had in common between us. I had been warming up to him even as I had been rationalizing his occasional insults. Enough was enough. Much as I wanted love, a relationship, a man in my life it felt to me that the price he was asking me to have was just too high for me to pay then. I had worked in a gender office before. Accepting intimate partner violence was not going to be my portion. So, back to my solace and celibacy it was.

Years later, my romantic life was going nowhere when a good friend suggested I give online dating a try. Unknown to her at the time I was a registered member of a few sites, nothing serious, but I would occasionally browse profiles and quickly sign off. I was even on one specifically for HIV positive people, which wasn't going very well- too much health information up front, too many painful stories, it was difficult to stay focused on the important stuff like "did we actually have anything in common, besides the health status." I was about to abandon this habit, because I was a half believer in this process. One day when scrolling I came across this profile on a regular site: a fine young guy, light brown skin, good pose, easy on the eye. We began conversing and months later agreed to an in-person meeting.

One of the trickiest thing of living with HIV, hands-down has been navigating the sex/dating scene and working to have a healthy sex life. In this regard, I've met a range of reactions to my open and honest disclosure of status. It's been the whole gamut- from "*oh, baby, that's not an issue*" followed by complete disappearance to "*hell, no! Woman, are you crazy? You want to infect me? Wait a minute- I probably am infected already, right? I'll sue you, B.....H!*"

Me: blink, blink. Just left standing there, to comfort myself.

I tell you no lies; that last line was one I actually heard from this guy months later. A real-life man living in the 21st century, with all of its information. I've resolved over the years that he belonged to that 25% that just can't take time to educate themselves and who allow their ignorance to fuel their actions, propelling all sorts of myths and certifying decade-old rumours that hurt people in their wake. We had done several in person weekends now, first he came over to my city and stayed the night then I reciprocated. It was all going good and I started to practice how I would word my disclosure to him. But before I came out fully to him, that saturday evening, as we were lying on his living room carpet, he got a bit too close and planted a huge kiss on my lips and squeezed me tight. What followed was nothing short of nasty. First a full disclosure of my status to him, followed by his ranting and raving, his threats to kick me out of his flat. But I knew no one else in his city, so where could I go for the night? I hadn't planned to stay in a hotel, having spent a lot already on the trip there.

"*Fine. OK. You can stay, just for the night, but I want you gone first thing in the morning!*"

"*Fine!*" I spat back. *Fine.* he resolved.

I made the first train home the following day, a sunday. I was disappointed, but it was understandable. What wasn't understandable was his whole reaction and course of action following that one encounter: an explosive letter to my doctor in all caps sent to him the following week in which he threatened to sue both my doctor and I if he were to test positive for HIV. This was after he and I had several telephone conversations and I relayed all the details of my medical health and condition; that I was on treatment, that the treatment was working and the viral infection was now suppressed and undetectable in my bloodstream, that I had been this way for years. It is during this chat that I divulged my doctor's number, actually recommending he have a talk with my general practitioner, a medical expert who had been following my health then for three years. I had presumed he would call the doctor, and be reassured about my health and feel safe, knowing that the likelihood of him getting an HIV infection from a person with an undetectable viral load was virtually negligible, as proved by the science at this time. Well, having worked in AIDS management and advocacy I knew this, had memorized statistics and shared them in various training rooms and forums. It was unfair to expect a newbie to this world to accept it all in such a short time, so I gave him space and time, with the offer to call me whenever he was confused or had questions. But I felt exposed and ashamed at my doctors when next I met him and apologized profusely, having to explain the entire situation and bare the painful contents of my life with this virus.

My doctor offered me no sympathy. To the contrary he assured me at my age I had no need for shame and had done nothing wrong. He reminded me that the duty to care, to protect was not on me; I did not have to bare my soul to every single man I came into contact with. I was taking on the role of caregiver in each of my intimate relationships when I needed caring for. It was time to stop taking on that role. It was simply my professional pride that had been scathed, nothing more. I sunk myself deeper into my work, daily hoping for a call from this man, some closure, anything. It never came. I chose to move on. I struggled to move on. I moved on.

You may judge me, thinking it was wicked of me not to say anything but it was early on in the relationship, I had every intent to disclose all. Most importantly also, I had been burned before. I had dated before, always with intent to share. In many jurisdictions knowingly infecting another with HIV is a criminal offence. So of course the bar I set for myself was very high, rarely getting myself into intimate scenarios where I would be moved to share my status meant I ran away from a lot of physical contact, and many interested suitors. At times even the ones I cared for and was attracted to. Simply because I could see that my status would be an issue. It pushed me to the point where it was all or nothing, and had meant at the time of disclosure I was too emotionally involved to be detached for their reaction to what I had to say. The problem with this approach meant I was always self conscious, checking myself a million times during some moments of intimacy, anticipating the next move, weighing the pros and cons of telling him now versus telling him later. It got exhausting. Sometime in 2010 I had had enough and just stopped sharing such private details (now public information), choosing instead to relax standards a little and to just go with the flow and enjoy a bit of tender love and care that was within safe guidelines. All efforts at disclosure after the fact seemed like taking advantage of the other, and I felt like I didn't have such tough skin, so it was back to celibacy for a while.

To avoid this hiccup in my romantic involvements yet another friend suggested I date only HIV positive men or men whose status I knew up front. The latter seemed even more exhausting, for how was I to obtain such info legally? So reluctantly, I agreed to see an HIV positive man she set me up with, Doug. This was in California. He was a gorgeous sandy-haired, blue eyed American guy with a good education and a sound private practice in his area of expertise. We hit it off great! Funny how after 10 years of being openly positive this was only the first time I was actually seeking this way of finding a life partner. Don't get me wrong, I wasn't desperate, I could take care of myself and pay my own bills. But a year prior my doctor had indicated these were some of my best years, to slow down, have a baby or two, as my health was still in good shape. Goal oriented me put that to the agenda, hence all these dates and rejections. For a very brief period time with Doug was easier than most relationships but just a few weeks in I got to learn that the thing I was so adamantly determined to have he may never give me. You see Doug did not want any children of his own, didn't want to spend a dime on any child and his opinion in fact was that the woman should be able to pay for any child she bears for this will protect many men from a lot of legal and financial troubles. Doug was a talented communicator and we had pretty amusing conversations about many things. The one thing that he definitely was also was not the settling kind, nor the man a reasonable woman decides to procreate with. On that note, in a few short weeks my heady, whirlwind, matchmade relationship with Doug was over, and a stronger relationship with myself blossomed. Each day in the shower or when listening to some good soothing music (mostly India.Arie or Nina Simone records at the time) wise words came to me. *Enough with loving everybody more. The only way I could move on was by loving myself more. I was certain of this- my past had taught me well. It was time to forgive myself any mistakes made and trust that I had love in my future at some point. Till then, I would leave these men alone. I was done with heartache and pain. Done with all the rejection. Done with all the planning and mental scenario creations. I was done kissing frogs!* Only time and laughter have helped to wipe away the pain of some of these encounters. I have many more that can fill a book. In hindsight, only laughter gives me comfort through these periods of my journey. Like Trevor Noah said, *"I always believe that funny is serious and serious is funny. You don't really need a distinction between them."*

A few weeks later I got a call from David, my now husband.

"How was the finance exam?" He remembered! I had once quickly rushed him off after a coffee meeting we had in Oakland, for old time's sake as former colleagues, as I saw my phone beeping a reminder- a *Finance Study Group meeting.* How we had come to have a coffee date in California when we had been working together for at least two years and never once dated is a story for another day. David's a gentle soul, a devoted Catholic and a man of inspiring patience and determination and a person I consider to be possibly one of the most remarkable Zambians you could get to know. He's an Ivy league trained health economist who has done some pretty awesome work, but most importantly he's a well rounded human being. What's ridiculous is how much time and effort I had spent into this entire mating process before it appeared that my husband and the father of my child was right there most of the time, right under my nose!

Chapter 9

✂ The ridiculous awesomeness that is Motherhood

I n the early weeks of winter, 2012 we were blessed with the gift of parenthood. I was awestruck to become a mother as it was both as unexpectedly joyful as motherhood is and quite sudden. It all happened so quickly. Of course we had been expecting the little guy, but not for a second had we anticipated the abrupt manner in which he entered our lives. Since knowing we were pregnant, we had done the obvious thing and sought supportive medical intervention in obtaining the prophylaxis to prevent mother-to-child transmission. So, the best story I will ever tell about my son's birth is that owing to gross early morning sickness and a pile of medication at my bedside each night and day, he was born HIV Negative! The worst story of his birth will forever be not about the alarming emergency c-section we agreed to in order To meet our first child, but the weeks and months following his birth, as he was born a premat at six and a half months of gestation. You read that right. Our son on the day of his birth that memorable friday afternoon weighed way less than a packet of sugar and required a full incubation unit and life support for weeks before we could take him home.

Owing to some slight abdominal pains and slight nausea, my husband and I had scheduled a checkup for me at the obstetrician just about 2 weeks before the birth. The doctor after careful examination informed us the baby was developing normally, and there was nothing out of sorts observed. He did, however, inform us that it looked like we would be having a "low weight baby", but he indicated this is no worrying matter, as babies gain weight in early weeks or early years. He had advised some bed rest and prescribed a follow-up visit a fortnight later at midday. A fortnight later, just before the afternoon lunch break my husband was to take at his office I took the bus ride into town. He and I met at our agreed upon location and proceeded by bus to the scheduled appointment. I felt supported in the entire pregnancy journey as my husband had been with me at all relevant hospital visits. On this particular friday in question he had just gotten back the day before from some duty travel so it felt especially warm and wonderful doing this visit together. He had been in the UK on official obligations but I had taken advantage of his visit to purchase a few maternity items to wear in the planned coming weeks. In fact we had planned to do somewhat of a pregnancy photoshoot that coming weekend as our "bump" had only just about started showing and I daily now wore the basic maternity jeans sold at the famous H&M store and tucked in my shirts, for added "pregnant woman effect". The elaborate photoshoot never happened. But I do have the one off picture of us standing proudly outside the maternity hospital in central geneva. We immortalized this moment before entering the obstetrician's office. He beckoned us in and showed me to the huge examination chair. *"So, Mrs Chipanta, how have you been and how are you feeling today?"*

"Oh great! I feel better than ever, the nausea is gone!" I was honestly cheery and feeling on top of the world on this day, with not a care at all.

He was usually a bubbly and chatty fellow, but on this day as he stared across his computer screen and listened to my ultrasound a quiet resolve and scowl formed on his face.

"Doctor?" My husband inquired.

"Hmmm. I am seeing something not quite right, but it is to do with an area not of my specialty. So, I will call and schedule an appointment for you right now, in this same building, on another floor. This guy is an expert in this area. He is the one that can confirm or dispute my findings."

"Oh, ok." We both looked at him with panic, but as I felt ten times better than I had 2 weeks prior I thought little of it. We took the elevator to the recommended specialist, who, without much fanfare, examined me and said to us he totally confirmed our obstetrician's findings, and for us to return to his office for next steps. By the time we returned to the first doctor it was clear several calls had been made and some directives were now available for us.

"It's lunch time, but Mrs. Chipanta I advise you not to eat anything solid right now, maybe perhaps you can pick up a drink or a yogurt, but nothing more. It's important that you both get to the hospital now and see this doctor. She will

be expecting you. She's an expert in these situations and will know how to handle you at this time. Please, go directly there, do not delay!"

My god! The alarm in his voice…, what had they found? My mind was racing. My husband and I walked swiftly to the bus station just downstairs and waited in silence for our corresponding bus to the indicated hospital. We were to be first time parents and didn't know if this was routine at this time or if we should be worried. We stopped briefly by the hospital cafe for me to grab a mulberry yoghurt on our way to the appointment. Well, I still had questions but I did not actually feel any fear until I saw a certain determined look exchanged between the recommended doctor X and my husband, after all the paperwork, examinations and insurance discussions had been exhausted. I was at this point lying on a hospital bed. I saw my husband and doctor X standing and in conversation at the foot of the bed. When she said to him out loud *"Ok! Your insurance is fine, I will proceed"*, my heart began to race. *Proceed with what? Where? How? What was going on? What had the doctors all seen?*

Doctor X came over, energetic and determined as ever. She instructed two assistants, then summoned another two, nurses I believe, to come by. They began pushing my bed and in a second, we were on the move! To the elevator they wheeled me and then through the doors. It was only once our entire party was there that doctor X spoke to me. In very carefully worded phrases she spoke to me.

"Madam, we are sorry. Your baby may have been having limited supply of oxygen or food, or both. This is why your obstetrician thought you may have a low weight baby. We can't be sure, but we think the baby's heart beat is getting weaker and weaker. If we wait and do nothing, we may not be happy with what we hear. Or, may not hear. So, today, right now, we are wheeling you into the theatre, I will aid you with a c-section and you will have this baby, today, right now."

What? Right now?!

As she said this one of the male nurses grabbed my hand and began slowly removing my rings and bangles. He placed them all in a brown envelope on which he had marked my name with a blue felt tip pen. Seeing my perplexed face he bent over to me and said *"these will be stored for you at reception. We will return them to your husband."*

At which point reality got to me. Yes! My husband! What had become of him? Someone explained that he had some paperwork to get through but he would soon join me in the theatre. That calmed me a bit. My heart was racing and my mind too, but I can't really say at this point I was scared. I suppose it is because I had absolutely no idea what to expect and had watched countless movies of babies being born and thought ok, women have c-sections often these days and what's the worst that could happen? It didn't dawn on me that at 27 and a half weeks our son was going to be two and a half months early and I didn't compute what that meant. I was on autopilot and numb with shock as they wheeled me into the operating theatre.

The room quickly got filled with the medical personnel, all donned in different colour uniforms, mostly blue, green and white. My husband walked in and was given his own greenish set of protective gear, which he quickly changed into in a nearby restroom. He came to my side of the theatre bed, the look of terror on his face, and we held hands. Not a word was said. My mouth was drying up and I had no words. Doctor X indicated we would start with a local anesthesia to my back. She also explained how all the various experts were in the room, in case of anything. My eyes darted around the room; 7 professionals spread out across the room with us. Then, she detailed how because our boy would be born a premat a neonatal specialist was present in the room and would take our newborn directly into an incubator and to the Intensive Care Unit as soon as he was born. We were told this was standard procedure in these sort of incidents. We nodded agreement and the anaesthetist came and sat behind me and began his work. Everything begun at 3:35 pm and I'll forever be delighted to say at some point after 4 pm, god's gift to me, my wonderful, special son came into this world, and much to my husband's surprise (even though we had been earlier notified) was quickly wrapped in foil and wheeled to the ICU of the maternity hospital. He didn't cry in the operating theatre, as babies do, and we had been told to expect this. But we received notification by a call that he had uttered some sound and all was progressing well in the ICU upon his registration. I was informed that as we had both had quite some dramatic events, we would both be left alone to rest and mother and baby, and dad could be reunited later in the evening.

I recall the esthetician reading me some rights, and mumbling something about what it would feel like when his medication wore off, and how I had the right to ask for morphine from the night nurse if I felt massive pain. We thanked him profusely and he left. I'll always remember his kind face and eyes, a person who surely must know how invaluable his work is to the planet! We were wheeled up to our room for the night and I slept like a log for a couple of hours. At ten pm that night we made our first visit to the ICU.

***Surviving ICU

It was seeing our baby for the first time that finally got me to register the emotion I am not too used to but that was obvious now: fear of the unknown. I stared at the feeble little guy with long arms outstretched, covered in aluminium foil, sleeping inside the glass incubator and felt sick to my stomach; like someone had just punched me. I could not utter a word, but just looked and blinked at him. Was I dreaming? Was this someone, or god's idea of a joke? I wanted this nightmare to end, for nothing about it was funny. My husband held me tight and squeezed my hand tighter. The vows we had casually exchanged on our wedding day in a very traditional catholic church in Lusaka, Zambia came to mind: *"for better or worse. In good times and in bad times…"*. *What type of time was this?* I firmed my lips shut tight together, and could feel my teeth sinking into the lower lip. We exchanged a scared, prayerful look. We both knew this one thing to be true: we needed God, the spirit, faith, a higher power to get through this hand that life had just dealt us. After sitting by our son's bedside for a bit the ICU quietened. I had been so preoccupied with our plight that I hadn't really taken in the full context of the room. We were in a ward just for premature babies in incubators, say about seven to ten babies. Some had their parents at their side like us, two weak everyday human beings who were now irreversibly joined in a life or death fight for the survival of their gift. I could see them, tense and fearful, but putting on a brave front as medical personnel came and went; issuing instructions, sharing their latest findings, giving strong directives but not quite stating whether in the end the little humans inside the glass structures would make it out of this ward safe and sound. Even for us, the medical personnel- from the doctor to the team of nurses, the nutritionist and even the receptionist were detailed about their methods and actions, but I noticed that they were very careful about the words they used; not wanting to give a total assessment of the child's prospect. Whenever we asked questions such as, *"But is our son going to be alright?"* or *"Do you think he will be well enough to come home with us in a week, a month?"* They never quite give straight answers, but nor did they dodge the question. I'll forever be indebted to the medical personnel and the fantastic Swiss health system for the wonderful way in which they handled our situation and supported our child through the most critical micro-minutes and months of his early development. In the early days of our pregnancy my husband and I had considered going elsewhere, to another country for the birth of our son, but his early arrival had precluded us from making this decision on time. But the way things played out we knew we had been at just the right place, for such a situation as this.

We retired to our room for the night, a room we had been assigned for the next three nights, for purposes of my post-natal recuperation. That first night, thoughts of my baby thin as a rod, and so pink and light that you could make out his veins swirled through my mind and got me to cry to sleep. At some point after two am I woke up to a sharp stabbing pain in my back. Why of course, the pain the aesthetician had warned me of. I grabbed some ibuprofen the night nurse had offered me earlier, but thirty minutes later the incessant throbbing pain was still there. Without hesitating I reached up to the bedside chord and pressed the special button I had been briefed on. I had forgotten so much else, but remembered that at the touch of this button a night nurse would be summoned, bearing the pain relieving morphine that I had a right to for this post operation recuperation. The nurse got into our room in no time. Only she was not bearing any medication, and in fact reprimanded me, saying the morphine would be given to me in drops to be determined by her and at intervals she saw fit, depending on the level of pain I was in. I heard her speak and hated the words coming out of her mouth. *"On a scale of 1 to 10, ten being extremely painful, how bad is the pain?"*

"A 7", I said, willing her to just inject the pain reliever into the drip.

"Oh ok. I'll administer the medication now."

She did the needful and sleep was just an eyelid shut away. The following night, though, much to my dismay, when I demanded this therapy we again went through this routine and she only came up with the medication, after three subsequent rings as the pain in my back lingered. On her last inquiry then I screamed, *"It's an eight! The pain is at an eight, please give me the drip."*

She gave me a small dose, and I thanked her. Much as she had been stern and precise about her measurements, I appreciated the work they were doing at this hospital. I also understood that medication as strong as morphine is not to be administered for long term use as it could lead to dependency and all manner of problems. On the day we finally left our assigned room I felt strong and proud thinking, am now a mom and have the evidence to show it: been through hell and back and am still here. When I relayed all this nightly drama to my husband I chuckled as I saw how clearly I too had been in extreme pain but concern for myself was almost nothing in comparison to the amount of care I put into our son's wellbeing. Yup, I was a mom!

In the mornings I would be wheeled from my maternity room to the ICU for visits to our son. Each time we were let in through the glass doors of the ICU I shed and held back tears. The fear was palpable and at times I would even feel the sense of shock in the other parents. It all got a little too real and scary on day three of our son's existence when they had to operate on his lungs and stomach for something that had gone wrong during birth. We were given so many details that I felt sick. I was appreciative of the thorough work of the medical team, but I would have rather not known any of the details of how the operation went awry and how they would redo it on day five. During this time we invited a priest to come pray over our son. My husband was in severe shock and I think at this point we both feared the worst outcome for the boy. On day six of our son's existence, one so far completely lived in glass case, a Catholic Father held a rosary in his hands, placed in our son's direction and prayed with us. He prayed fervently for the boy's life to be spared, but then again he prayed strongly for god's will to be done. The three of us stood around the incubator thereafter in stone cold silence before the priest left for possibly his next dutiful call of the day. My husband and I would take turns doing the visits and in a week, when he was released from intensive care we took turns to practise his kangaroo feeding. I must say what was incredibly helpful at this time was a special room we had been assigned, a private wing set aside specifically for parents of premats that was a private part of the maternity wing that few knew about. It is a donated wing and over the years has served to provide many families like ours who were in dire straits with subsidized accommodations whilst caring for a sick infant. The room had a television, a bath and toilet and even a little kitchenette, complete with a microwave and one plate stove that we could cook in. But after the daily bath I spent most of my time either atop the bed, praying or sleeping, or by the foot of the bed, praying or crying. During this time my ipad was a constant companion, relaying a playlist of uplifting music, mostly gospel, to get me through the days. Three songs I had on repeat on that playlist were songs titled *"That's what faith can do" by the gospel group Kutless, "Steady my heart" by legendary gospel artist Kari Jobe and "Stronger" by famous past Idol show contestant Mandisa,* all pure gold in my view! Whenever possible I also scribbled random thoughts into my notes and journaled the experience. Somehow I got into a creative mode and also wrote the final bits of my first novel around the second week of this stay. I also happened to find an arts and crafts store at the corner of the maternity wing and purchased a brand new knitting set, with which I began daily poking at until, months later the outline of what looked to be a scarf showed up. The object of my knitting had no name, I just knitted and knitted daily, practising each twist and turn with the needles and adding more and more vibrant colours til a daily satisfaction point was reached. A latent skill, picked up in one home economics class I had taken in the fifth grade, was clearly still there! This and the belief that god would *"never leave me, nor forsake me"* are what got me through this most bizarre, draining and difficult of circumstances. After two weeks of this special accommodation we continued monitoring our son's progress by visiting the children's hospital from home. Our son, now off life support, but still unable to fully breathe or eat on his own was placed in what they call the Neonatal Development Unit, with others similar to him. It is during this time, whilst on a coffee break or waiting in the reception area that I met and connected with other preemie moms. Some of these have remained in close contact, and with some we have become real-good friends, watching our premature kids grow together and break every milestone set on them. I remain thankful for each of these connections, and it is in concert with some of these parents that I have been involved in fundraising initiatives to support premats. We organize fundraisers and use the proceeds to purchase clothing or needed materials to premats and hospital wards taking care of preemies. It is in conversations with some of these parents that I would eventually find comfort and utter my deepest anguish and pain and thoughts about the experience we had all gone through. If I didn't lose my mind at some point along this journey it is credit to one or more of these mothers who would cry with me and say *"Hey, me too! I've hated every part of this experience and stayed up at night with similar worries."*

Knowing that we were ordinary people forced to go through such extraordinary things made me stronger. At times, it seemed to me like God as creator had let me in on his little secret project of how he makes humans. To watch my little boy twitching behind the glass or struggle to suck eight millilitres was literally like being witness to a miracle! Where once there was doubt came a re-invigorated faith. For weeks all we had was the frame of a little human, but one day, on about his fourth week of existence, at last, I saw what seemed to me like the face of a very healthy baby. I took and saved this photo of the boy and todate it remains a first and lasting memory of this experience, as all other images taken prior were somehow not automatically backed up on the ipad and we mourned their demise. One fine sunny day, after three months in the unit we were told our son was ready to come home with us.

***Preemie at home

Taking our little bundle of joy home came with its encumbrances. First, he had to fit in the car seat we had been assigned to provide on the day of his hospital release. Then, when leaving the hospital it was as if we still had a critical patient to care for as documents were signed and lots of medical items given to us for home use- hand sanitizers, masks, thermometers. But we took it all in stride and were just overjoyed with the transition. Our boy had undergone so many scans, including brain, ear, eyes, nose examinations that we saw this moment as a great win. But once home the medical system did not completely abandon us. We had what the swiss call *"les infirmiers a domicile"*, or nurses at home service visit us twice a week. They came to monitor his eating and breathing and each week the little baby was placed on a scale to check for any weight gain. At first it was all great news and quick bursts of growth. But then suddenly the little fellow fell sick and caught what they informed us was a bout of meningitis and had to be hospitalized again. At this time my mother-in-law had come to visit us from Zambia and she was really sad about this eventuality, saying *"perhaps it is me. Perhaps it is my coming. I hope I didn't infect him"*. As we had been warned that he was very susceptible to many infections at this point we had kept many away. Our friends and co-workers had not yet come to see him. The few who entered our home had to sanitize and wear face masks in order to get close to our boy. The time taught us so much about how not to question science and to just do the needful. For us there was nothing strange about this, it was just the way it was. The boy spent about another couple of weeks in hospital before his final joyful return home. During this time we also applied faith to all of our actions. We had been through the hospital doors before, but we didn't want to take any step, any day for granted. So we this time invited our cousin, another Catholic Priest, Father Chongo, based out of the Vatican in Rome, Italy, to visit us and pray for the boy. One of my sisters, Tael, also visited about this time. Having family around really soothed our pain and reminded us we could still laugh and focus on other matters, even throughout this most trying time. We resolved once he was home to slowly ease into a more normal existence, but with precautions still as by now the baby was just about six months old. We invited some few friends over and eventually most of our associates got to come home and pray with us or simply spend a minute to know and appreciate the gift of life we had been blessed with. In total by this time our son had been seen or attended to by well over sixty medical personnel. In a completely surprising outcome and one I call a true work of God, our son triumphed over each challenge and met every milestone from this time on. We clearly had a little warrior on our hands and resolved to do our best to raise him right. In the past eight years since his birth he has yet again succumbed to all manner of illness; dry skin, eczema, and many frantic episodes of illness. We've just had to grow in parental grace for these times and have gotten to accept that this is the way it is, the deal with raising a living, breathing human infant. There are grand, majestic times and then there are valley moments when we don't understand what is happening, but still we remain cognizant of the wonder of a life bestowed upon us. It is what it is, but it's mostly a good and joyous gift.

Prematurity is a growing global phenomenon and one that still requires much awareness raising. We all can join in too in a real simple way, no money required: just save the date November 17th in your calendar as the Premat International Day. Wear purple, talk about it, raise awareness in your own way. Premature babies come into this world facing so many challenges. Whatever we can all do to help them cope better gives peace to many.

***GIRL GANG

"Girls come into this world to win too. They want to compete, to perform, to throw those punches. Girls want to get ahead too."

I was in that Parisian crowd in April, 2019 when the uber-fabulous former First Lady of the United States Michelle Obama said those words. I remember myself mouthing the words with her on-screen reflection thereafter: "*...And those girls become women. Those girls are us.*" YAY, the crowd clapped loudly and I was a part of it, awestruck and giddy with excitement at her presence on the huge stage. I had taken the early morning train to Paris. Seeing as her Book tour for "Becoming" did not show Geneva as a stop city I had resolved to get myself a ticket at the nearest city as soon as tickets went up for online purchase. The beauty of the modern tech world. Online ticket in hand it didn't take me long to also secure a ride into and out of Paris for the night of the event, easily done, with a lovely new tech invention known as Blahblahcar, a quick ride provider that offers you cheap and available seats on those travelling between popular european cities. I managed to arrange a bus ride for the return. With that done, I marked the date on all my calendars- the digital, the one hanging on our kitchen wall, to the left of the stove (so I can glance at each month's entries as I prepare the family evening meal), and the phone one. Grown women like me, one would ask why such an event was such a big deal to me. Well, firstly- its MO- Michelle Obama, queen of everything; the first black american first lady of the famous United States; mom to two gorgeous black daughters, wife to the notable former president, trained lawyer and in fact, to date, the most educated first lady of said country. Might I add she is both brilliant and well-spoken. How could one not jump at a chance to be in the same room with her (even if separated by several aisles and screens?). I had to go! Secondly, this was the sort of event I turn to to remind myself what a girl I am; how I still have passions worth pursuing. Many of my girlfriends have shared an interest in a similar pursuit: baking, learning to cook, registering for the same annual retreat, travelling with their kids or alone when possible or sightseeing and hiking into the woods when not with their better half. Call it escaping or what you may, but it's a woman's recognition that she is more than just a label that society places on her and that she can be and do more than what each role she plays necessitates. For me I have found over the years am very guarded about my right to dream and also to express myself freely in society as I chose. It's not rebellion; it's the right to self-determine, to identify oneself as belonging to this group, or that school of thought or that club; all which are like breathing to me. There is a part of every person, surely where one can be them, just them, with no attachments, without this being disrespectful or seen to be disowning every other aspect of one's societal obligations. You see, we women, we girls, we all know this and that's one you may have heard of the "Women's code" or Girl code. Having read so much about this I know there are so many rules that exist and I adhere to neither, but I do know that I have a Girl Gang and that without it, without each of the various young, savvy, energetic, sophisticated women that form this gang that I wouldn't have made it through all the challenges and grand moments of this life. Especially through motherhood. Granted, motherhood is an almost lonely experience that every woman faces in her own unique way, and yet as mothers we have similar stories and can bond over what our unique journey was like. I have cherished candid moments with girlfriends at lakeside picnics, sharing a bottle of red wine whilst venting over our frustrations and fears over our children. I recall book club meetings, dinner reservations, evening walks with girlfriends over which we were all able to disclose what was irking us and gain insight on how a friend had navigated a similar circumstance and overcome. Whilst it isn't always about irritations with one's husband, I'll admit, there's at times a bit of that, c'est la vie, marriage is a beautiful, but not an easy feat! But a huge part of my interactions with girlfriends has really been bonding over the question of how will we continue to express ourselves fully, as women, workers, wives, mothers, sisters, neighbours and so on whilst remaining true to our beings, our calling? Mind you- my girl gang is rather diverse, so am not just talking about my black women friends, or those I hang out with who are also HIV positive. My girl gang is a rainbow collection of dynamic, educated, empowered, well-read, well-travelled, highly-engaged women who are all very much alert through life and contributing to society's advancement through their various professional profiles and crafts. My friends are lawyers, bankers, doctors, entrepreneurs, activists, artists and also women who chose to not be identified by what they do in life. True to the core of who I am, I also have friends who live and work in the informal economy; they have chosen this life or it has chosen them; they may never be seen, and that's ok. I define a friend as someone loyal to me, with whom I share a particular bond and history and from whom I am able to glean some wisdom. So, with some friends I have been blessed to enter fine restaurants in Lilongwe, Lusaka, Paris, Brussels, Amsterdam, Geneva with, and yet, with others a tall glass of water shared on a mat in their backyard will do. Remember Verity, my mother, the peacemaker? She taught me that you always need a friend- in high places and in other places. Now as an adult I understand. I understand how and why I have a friend for every season. There's the friend who is a socialite and I can call on when I throw a party and need someone to keep guests entertained. There's the friend to call in an emergency because she'll know what to do and say. There's the friend to share the best news with first who loves to celebrate and plan a good time. Then there's the friend who will lend a non-judgemental, listening ear when I am exhausted and tearful and going on about fatigue with my life-long medication regimen. Then there is also the need for discernment as to who will be comfortable with whom in a group, as not all friends need to be bunched up like a bouquet. All lovely and wonderful, all for a reason and a season, just like the prettiest of flower petals. We find ourselves in another, and at times meet the side of us we often keep tucked away. This is a lesson I hope to transfer onto my son, and already see it budding in him. I recall entering this year, the notorious ad now memorable 2020 with family. Then a few days later making time so my son and I could spend an hour outdoors with a friend and her kids outdoors. Truth be told we had missed each other and badly wanted to share that cup of "mama juice" as we call it and share new year goals and aspirations. So, to the park she carried a huge bottle of something bubbly and I brought along my plastic goblets. Sante! We screamed in each other's ears, giggling and sipping away, licking sticky liquid off our fingers as our teenage selves would. In that brief encounter, in those intimate moments our inner girl spark was re-ignited and we once again got to meet who we are on the inside. Such moments can only be refreshing, and ought to be scheduled in and repeated over and over as often as one can. That girly glow is so needed, even in the most serious of us all. Life as a full grown woman on planet earth demands it.

It's been these girly times, or the mom life that has kept me centred and sane through the years.

Chapter 10

A digital nomad

"To make an embarrassing admission, I like video games. That's what got me into software engineering when I was a kid. I wanted to make money so I could buy a better computer to play better video games - nothing like saving the world".

-Elon Musk

We all live in a tiny global digital village now. It is either loved or hated, or tolerated. Either way, we didn't choose it; it chose us.

The internet has made our world so small, online business such a huge possibility and offered us all so many great chances to begin again, brand ourselves anew, identify ourselves again, share our skills. As I pursue this entrepreneurial journey I know it is as fragile and yet as harsh as living with HIV is, and there is a comfort in that: no guarantees, no assurances; just the day-to-day journey of hope, trust and doing my best daily to grind away. In 2016 I fulfilled an amazing dream I had for a short time- that of launching my own design of perfume. During the short time in San Francisco, California I had met an incredible bunch of female creatives through a group of Latina women interested in pushing themselves further along in life and business. At one of their sessions I met a dynamic, fired up, beautyboss- an American woman who owned her own fragrance production studio, and who offered training and a small business consulting opportunity. What can I say? The rest is history! Following my sign up, training and purchase of their starter kit I began making and selling handcrafted perfumes; first under their brand, and later under mine: BU by Bhatupe. Fast forward to today- my business remains small, as I find joy in the slow and mostly natural hand production of goods, producing a couple of tens or hundreds of items at a time, aiming to cultivate a niche. I sell via website, social media, select fashion boutiques, pop-up stores and events and the greatest business lesson I have learned so far is so similar to my life lesson: let it surprise you! Contrary to my expectations at times I find those who seem to have money don't buy and those you are unsure of may end up being very loyal customers. This has kept me going, even during slow times, as the joy and happiness of a satisfied customer and the realization that something I created sets off such good vibes is such a huge motivation. What started off as a small spark has taken me to super exclusive, luxe events in Milan, Italy, such as the annual *Exsence Festival*, and to Amsterdam, where I've mingled with and learned from some of the most progressive minds in olfactory and creative spaces. The ultimate joy in being a creative is that one also becomes a new person as layers are peeled off, newness within is revealed. I love it! When I am making solid perfume, or blending natural oils for a client for a personalized scent I relax and take in my new identity as a creative and know that am more than just a statistic: HIV can take a seat.

The other area in which I currently cultivate and find joy is in work with other young creatives, specifically tech enthusiasts. As I pursued my MBA back in the day in California one thing that was clear was that I was beaten by the tech bug by the end of the program. Here I was studying in california, the home of Apple and Steve Jobs and with our campus so close to Silicon Valley my entire class in fact got to meet and hear from the notable Apple co-founder, Steve Wozniak at one of our campus events [I was then serving as Vice President for the Campus Business Challenge that year and got to welcome Mr. Wozniak at reception and walked him to the event room]. In past work I had made huge use of the internet of course, and even managed websites, updating software, making use of javascript and basic functionalities (with the dependability of an IT unit, of course). But here I was in class daily with real IT nerds, engineers, programmers who at times spoke mostly in code. They rattled off words like IOS, Google Play, Android, pay-per-click, Samsung versus Apple war...my ears grew bigger and the curious cat that I was, I wanted to learn more. So I signed up for and tuned in more eagerly into a course we eventually had that year: Strategic Management of IT, in which the lecturer got super technical on us all and made me eager to learn code. Little did I know I was wading in the water and nearing the deep end of a very turbulent ocean. I explored, I sampled, I toyed with a few online courses before realizing one needs an entire PHD in Computer Science and hours of study and the famous "10,000 hours" as put forward by Mr. Jobs, to make any real impact in this world. I carried on with my other life goals, not sure where this newfound interest fit in.

Today it's very clear where this passion has been of use to me. I see technology not only as a vehicle for developmental transformation, but also as an entry point for more equality in society and as one of the most key areas where individuals, governments and societies have to invest energy and resources in the coming years. We're in a global village and soon it will almost not matter whether one is living in Dedza, Malawi, or in New Delhi: with a wifi connection and high-speed internet, and various offline services working well many young people will make a huge impact on the planet and we'll know their names. This realization is what got me eventually signed up two years ago as an Ambassador for the Swiss Tech Incubator known as Seedstars[13]. Seedstars brings together investors for the US and Europe and runs an annual competition in which they source innovation from around the world. In 2017 I was in their audience at their annual gathering in Lausanne when they talked of their desire to increase sourcing in "emerging countries". Africa was on their mind, and following the impressive, screen-filled presentations and music I made my way around the networking zone and found their focal point for Africa. *Question?* I blurted out, nerve-excitedly. *"Yes, sure. What's up?"* Claudia, the Seedstars Rep for Africa responded. *"Are you guys operational in Malawi? I see Kenya, Nigeria here. Do you source techies also from there? That's my country. I am Malawian. I know a few young people doing good…"* A conversation started. In that first year, I was asked to make a case; build reasons for Seedstars expansion into Malawi. What was in it for them? What sort of tech ecosystem did the country have? Who were the major players? How many hubs were present? What challenges were the young people working to counter? On and on it went. Never afraid of the work tied to an opportunity, I got cracking! I reached out to entrepreneurs I knew, set up some digital forums, got excited about creating a movement for investment and visibility for this space. Silence. Not much was coming back to me. During one family holiday I passed through Lilongwe for a few days, visited the local tech hub, Mhub, spoke with their founder, Racheal Sibande, a contemporary from my college days. A spark. An outline of areas of work that were daunting, a discovery

---

[13] www.seedstars.com

of the remarkable achievements that could be made in collaboration rather than competition. Finally, I saw it clearly: my role was simply that of the bridge-builder. I got back to Geneva reinvigorated, with a list of innovations and founders who were determined and wanting to occupy global tech spaces. In 2018, at last, following a policy change in its operations Seedstars opened up access to Malawi. You'll find their annual reports informative of this period. It was early days, not much came out of that year. But last year, at last Seedstars physically made it into Lilongwe, Malawi, hosted the first ever local pitching contest, the winner of which was supported to attend their regional contest in Johannesburg, South Africa. Emmanuel, the Founder of OCLIYA, a healthtech app emerged strong and determined to continue building his invention even though Malawi did not qualify for either of the 10 coveted spots from African region that made it to the final contest in Lausanne, Switzerland each year. But we were there! For a few minutes while he presented on stage and I sat beaming from ear to ear in that audience in South Africa our country name and flag stood brightly on a huge screen: MALAWI. The work continues, and am certain one of these days huge strides and *glocal* innovation by a young Malawian techy will be noted by the Seedstars community and world, as many other huge talents have already been discovered. But, most importantly, it's already happening. If covid has taught us anything it is that making products locally is beneficial to economies in this new world order and that if those products can be globally-relevant in nature, design, and utility then the sky's the limit as to what can be accomplished. In the first few months of covid we're already seeing young engineers making wearable masks using 3D printing technology, safe-contact soap dispensers, for example. It's here! The advanced future we were all told of is already here and will keep on pushing us to adapt further.

As I do this work- of networking, sourcing, collaborating, and seeking investor pools to grow this ecosystem I also disappear into the new assumed role. For it is in becoming something new that we let go of what we once were. In my case, of course I'll never stop being an HIV-positive person, for this is a lifelong relationship (please laugh!), but it's totally liberating to be more than just that. I am an enabler, a contributor, a bridge-builder to others' dreams, and to my own dream of wanting to make a small difference in my corner of the world.

These days when I get up in the morning and start scratching off items on the to-do list- be it mothering, business demands, calls with young techies, working on being a good wife, or simply writing this book am cultivating joy in each moment, counting my blessings and just busy about the living. These days, with yet another global pandemic looming, we are all simply dying to live.

Epilogue

You never know what people are going through, no matter how gorgeous or well put together they seem. You may have read all those famous books on how to turn your life around. This is not one of them. Clearly, there are so many situations, like mine, in which the adversity never leaves us immediately. No. We are forced to live with the negative outcomes of some big, bad or unfortunate decision that we made at some point in time. The situation may be big or small. The "thing" you live with may be noticeable or invisible to others. But you know it's there. Change doesn't always come instantly either, at times taking an entire lifetime to show up. My belief is that once you "own it", whatever your vice is, accept it and find ways to go around it, without bowing to its shame or dismissing its presence then you are ready; really ready for your next, best life! I don't believe in that whole big turn around thing. Well, maybe in financial loss issues this rings true. You lose a house when you reach rock bottom and you may be fortunate and buy three more houses later on in life. But these will not be the same home you once bought, for a house is not a home. I may be belabouring the point. To end? Embrace yourself: flaws and all. Present you. Show up as you. Be You.

But you may be there reading this and saying, *"girl, woman, lady, shah! You have no idea what my circumstances are like….how bad things are for me."* Try me! I am living with and have lived with, for almost two decades now, a tiny incurable virus that most of the world fears and that many will rather not even mention; one for which the world is yet to discover a vaccine, and it's been over 30 years of this response. But the thing that flabbergasts me the most? Now, years later, almost without hesitation I am able to write that, say that, scream it out loud if I have to. Not only to you. To them. I'll say it to whoever is in the room and wherever necessary. It doesn't matter who's in there with me. It matters that if my purpose demands it, am there to repeat it. I know that this saves lives. Contrast this with my response in the first 6 months of knowing this positive diagnosis. I was devastated. I spoke of this three-letter worded virus only in whispers. Each time I did so I swear I broke out into a sweat and shook just a little. When I saw a roadside poster on this I felt naked, exposed and wanted to run for the hills, but where to go? With HIV being such a worldwide phenomena it was hard to imagine a city where such banners didn't exist. Over time this feeling dissipated. I never planned to ever talk of my experiences or share any of this news publicly. It just happened. As I willed myself deeper and deeper into finding meaningful ways to spend my life before it was soon over I found myself drawn to charitable organizations, got involved and one thing led to another and am here. Am here to remind you that things are not as bad as they seem and that if you just keep focused on what's good, what's working, on what you are blessed with a colourful life will unfold before you and you will bask in its glow and wonder what happened and how it happened. Life can be challenging when we list a million things we want to make our dreams a reality. But have you ever thought of what you would actually do with a reality that is exactly as you dreamt? Well, maybe not exactly but close to what you fully desire? Let's just pretend daily that we have this desired outcome. Will you do that now? Will you wake up each morning and count first things first- you have breath, you are alive, you have a new day ahead! Then, can you just hold that approach to living all through the day- focusing on what's good, what you still have, who you have beside you, what small thing is working out? Cause believe you me, there is no secret to lasting joy and happiness in this life but that. Robert Holden Ph.D, in this book *Happiness Now!: Timeless Wisdom for feeling good fast* writes:

"You enjoy as much happiness as you believe you're worthy of...the more self-acceptance you have, the more happiness you'll allow yourself to accept, receive, and enjoy."

This phrase "dying to live" has been with me for over a decade. I listed many things I would rather have happened before I died. In the earlier days of diagnosis I was convinced death was just months away. Having goals kept me *too "busy to have that happen right away"*. As if any of us can escape death. Over the years the resolve has become so strong that eventually HIV had to take a backseat. I still do those routine checkups and blood draws, contribute my results to scientific surveys and follow many HIV-positive rights organizations online. Since that first diagnosis I have taken thousands, and still take the daily pills. I just aim to not make this the main thing. It stopped being the thing that defines my entire life. Each daily pill I take at the end of each privileged day is a reminder of just how fortunate I have been, when so many millions succumbed to this vice. I am a product of our times, and am always enthusiastic to make use of all resources at all our disposal in this digital age to up my positive (all pun intended!) and down all the negatives. And you can too. Wake up! See the world! Look around you! It's not all bad. I assure you, whatever hardship you are facing right now: you are bigger than this. You can rise up. Small steps matter! One day you will tell your story and guess what? You will not cry whilst doing it either. It's possible for any of us to turn our tragedies into life-giving stories of triumph.

It's been my experience these past 18 years that as we are all living til we die we have to aim to be dying to live when we lose zeal and gusto. And when the flame in us fades a little, when our smiles are momentarily wiped away we've got to get to that place where we know we are able to count at least one thing that's going good; because there always is something to be grateful for! Because anything less is not worthwhile. Anything less means losing the will to live.

In so many ways then I end to say paradoxically, life and the living are a fight. Sometimes it is peaceful and we can go easy and enjoy it. But when our very existence is put at risk, we must gather courage within by finding something, anything worth fighting for.

So daily then I live an HIV positive life. It's not a piece of cake, nor is it any longer the "death sentence" it was so many years ago. There are millions of people like me right this minute who are living daily with HIV. Just as we have seen there is no cure as yet for Covid19, for the past 3 decades the world has been in hot pursuit of the AIDS vaccine, to no avail. As both epidemics plague the earth it's clear we need to urgently act to eradicate both viruses. One can only hope that with these lockdowns and the 'new normal' that access to HIV preventative tools will scale up too. Because if not done soon millions will succumb to either, or both viruses. For now though all I can hope for is that you, dear reader, would put down this book and consider taking your own HIV test whilst you also mask up. It could mean everything for your life and that of those you love. Stay safe!

With mom in Maputo, Mozambique, aged 6

With my Ethiopian neighbours and friends
playing outside in Lusaka, Zambia

At KAF Headquarters, Cologne-Bonn, Germany, 2003

With my sister Grace in New York city, 2008

With former UN Secretary General, Dr. Kofi Annan

with Former UNAIDS Executive Director, Dr. Piot (right)
and Barbara Bush, founder, Global Health Corps

With former Secretary General of the United Nations Ban Ki-Moon

With my family at the Eiffel Tower, Paris, 2019

With degree in hand, Chancellor College, 2002

With my friend and spiritual mentor, Susan Sanson

Glossary

Portuguese to English

Batatas Fritas- French fries
Camarão- Shrimp
Cerveja- Beer
Trinta tres andares- Building in Maputo, Thirty three stories high

Chichewa to English

Chitenje (noun)- Colourful piece of cotton cloth mostly worn by women in traditional settings

Nsima- traditional staple in southern africa, known by many names, made of corn.
Nkhuku yowamba- Smoked chicken
Masamba wotendela- Vegetables in a peanut butter stew
Mesho- College slang term for room mate

Swahili- English

Matatus- minibuses

Abbreviations

PLHIV - person or people living with HIV

Printed in the United States
By Bookmasters